OPEN ADOPTION: RESEARCH, THEORY AND PRACTICE

For Megan

Open Adoption: Research, Theory and Practice

MURRAY RYBURN

Avebury

Aldershot·Brookfield USA·Hong Kong·Singapore·Sydney

30141427

Published by
Avebury
Ashgate Publishing Limited
Gower House
Croft Road
Aldershot
Hants GU11 3HR

Ashgate Publishing Company
Old Post Road
Brookfield
Vermont 05036
USA

British Library Cataloguing in Publication Data

Ryburn, Murray
    Open Adoption: Research, Theory and
    Practice
    I. Title
    362.734

ISBN 1 85628 692 4

Printed and Bound in Great Britain by
Athenaeum Press Ltd, Newcastle upon Tyne.

Contents

4 Research into contact and permanent placement

Part II: Experiences of openness

5 Lorette

6 Chris and Joanne

7 Lois, Taff and Selina

Acknowledgements

My special thanks are due to Lorette, Chris, Joanne, Lois, Taff, Selina, Matthew, Annabel, Lynne, Andrea, Sarah, Neil, Robin, Charlotte, Maria, Marc and Gina for sharing their adoption stories.

Thanks also to Mary Ryan for comment on a draft of chapter one to Liz Ryburn for proof reading of a first draft and initial work on the index, and to Barbara Fletcher for general review, comment, proof reading and final compilation of the index.

Introduction

This book is concerned with the research into and theory of identity formation, the specific issues of identity posed for all parties in adoption, and with law, research, policy and practice in relation to open adoption. The discussion and arguments are grounded in the experiences of those who are parties to adoption. Its focus is on children and young people who are adopted by strangers rather than those adopted by relatives. Its principal claim is that good professional practice must always centre on entrusting or restoring to consumers of adoption services the fullest possible decision-making role, and that to do so is to challenge much of prevailing theory and practice.

Despite a decline from 24,831 adoptions in England and Wales in 1968 (Houghton Report, 1972, p.122) to a present figure of just over 7,000 adoptions a year (Adoption Law White Paper, 1993, p. 4) adoption is the focus of intense media interest and public and professional debate.

This abiding interest in adoption stems in part from the fact that there have been more than 800,000 adoptions in England and Wales since 1926, of which half a million have been non-familial adoptions by strangers. When we add to this number the many relatives of adoptees, both by birth and adoption, then it is a matter that directly concerns a sizeable proportion of the population. Research indicates (see below chapter four) that for adopted people and both their original and their adoptive families adoption remains a significant fact which may assume great importance at various points in the life cycle (see for example Brodzinsky *et al*, 1992). It is this life-time nature of adoptive status and the relationships it forges, in combination with an incidence of primary and secondary infertility that is now estimated to affect as many as one in six couple relationships, that will continue to keep adoption in the public domain and on health and social services agendas.

Adoption is not only an issue for those whom it affects directly. The practice of adoption challenges ideas about the nature of family and the relative weighting that should be accorded to social kinship in comparison with biological kinship. It provokes debate about the role of the State in family matters, and brings into question not only assumptions about the best interests of children but also the qualities necessary if they are to be parented effectively. Finally, adoption calls on us to consider the relationship between altruism and self-interest, nature and nurture, difference and conformity.

Where the State intervenes in family matters its mandate for doing so is almost always ambiguous, reflecting as it does competing wishes for social order and individual choice. Adoption, and the practice that flows from it, is a microcosm of this tension. It is a major intrusion by the State into the sanctity of the family; it is a victory for social order over biological kinship.

The inherent tension that stems from socially constructing families has often been denied in adoption law, policy and practice in England and Wales. These instead have tended to centre on the myth of a wholly new beginning for children and young people, separated forever, to all intents and purposes, from their origins. This book maintains that the tension between biologically and socially constructed families is a fundamental and inescapable feature of any form of legal adoption. Legislators, policy makers and practitioners cannot frame law, policy and practice to avoid this tension, except by deluding themselves at a potential cost for those who are parties to adoption.

In many respects adoption can be seen as a denial of the fact that we inhabit a society where most of us are able to take change and the renegotiation of important aspects of our lives for granted. In general our practice in adoption creates a divide for adopted people between the past and present which is often difficult, and sometimes impossible to bridge.

By contrast open adoption includes the planned and conscious maintenance of links between those who are adopted and their original family networks. These links may take many forms and may be sustained by letter, telephone, video and audio recording as well as direct contact. The services of an intermediary may be used to facilitate links or they may be directly maintained by the parties themselves.

Open adoption requires open models of practice, practice based on a belief that the best decisions in the lives of those who use adoption services will be the ones they make for themselves. Where this belief underpins law, policy and practice, outcomes may be essentially different from those where the key decisions are taken by professionals on behalf of service users. The principal point of departure from traditional practice lies in the potential for parties to sustain and negotiate relationships in ways that 'normalise' them, and which take account of changing needs and circumstances. Where decisions have already been taken on behalf of others, the aim of an open practice model is to restore to them a major say in any future decisions.

The advantages of open adoption emerge most clearly in the views and experiences of parties to adoption which are at the centre of this book. They form a framework for the examination of the different issues posed by openness and open practice in relation to legislation, the research, theory, policy and practice.

Where necessary, I have used the term adoptee rather than the rather clumsy she/he, though I am aware that this may have a depersonalising effect.

Part I: Research and theory in open adoption

1 The law, the judiciary and openness

Introduction

This chapter examines the legislation on continuing contact between the parties in adoption from the time of the 1958 Adoption Act to the present day. It considers the relationship between the Children Act and adoption legislation, and the attitude of the judiciary to contact in adoption. It concludes by examining the question of whether greater openness in adoption is primarily an issue for the law and the courts or for practice.

Access to birth records before the Children Act

Although Scotland permitted adopted people who had reached seventeen access to birth records from the time of the passing of its first adoption legislation in 1930, in England and Wales, under section 11(7) of the 1926 Act, this was not so unless there was a court order permitting it. There was, however, open access to identifying information at the time of court proceedings and this right remained until the passage of the 1949 Adoption Act, and the consolidating Act of 1950, which at section 3(3) stated that consents could be given without the disclosure of the identity of the adopters. In Scotland access to records for adoptees aged over seventeen continued from 1930 to the present. According to Triseliotis (1991) the origins of this provision lay in a wish to facilitate inheritance from original families.

The significant inequality in the different jurisdictions from 1950 was not addressed until 1975 in England and Wales, and 1987 in Northern Ireland. The Houghton Committee (1972), whose recommendations were largely incorporated in the new legislation, did not initially recommend birth records access in their working paper published in 1970, but they finally conceded to the weight of opinion which supported opening up records. In their report (1972, para. 303) they say that "The weight of evidence as a whole was in favour of freer access to background information and this accords with our wish to encourage greater openness about adoption". Triseliotis's study, *In Search of Origins* (1973), commissioned by the Committee, was particularly instrumental in highlighting the negative consequences of secrecy for some adoptees.

The Adoption Act 1976, incorporating provisions of the 1975 Children Act, at section 51 provides that the "Registrar General shall on application ... by an adopted person ... who has attained the age of 18 years supply to that person ... such information as is necessary to enable that person to obtain a certified copy of the record of his birth". There is provision that those adopted before 12 November 1975 attend a counselling interview before the release of a birth certificate. This was an attempt to address the issue of giving retrospective information to adoptees in circumstances where their birth parents may have understood their relinquishment decision always to be confidential. There is no legal provision, however, that can cover circumstances where adopted people search their origins without using or formally seeking access to official records.

Adoption Agencies also have a general power under the Adoption Agency Regulations 1983 (regulation 15) to disclose any information that they hold, should such disclosure be seen as necessary for the discharge of their functions as an agency within the meaning of the Adoption Act. These functions are prescribed in the general duty in section 1 of the Act for all local authorities to "establish and maintain a service designed to meet the needs, in relation to adoption", of children who have or may be adopted, their parents or guardians, or any who have adopted or may adopt a child. One of the principal difficulties with a power such as this, expressed in the broadest terms, is that while it allows considerable scope for agencies to disclose information, it is also susceptible to a wide variety of interpretations.

In the absence of clearer guidance, it is the beliefs, attitudes and values of individual practitioners that are likely to be key determinants of what information is shared from agency records. Whilst in some cases adopted people report being given very free access to information on files, in other instances philosophies of secrecy, confidentiality and protection seem to prevail, and minimal information is shared.

Changes in access to records under the Children Act
The Adoption Act 1976 was amended by the Children Act 1989, and a new section, 51A, establishes a Contact Register. This provision commenced on 1 May 1991, and it places a duty on the Registrar General to maintain a register of adopted persons aged over 18 years and their relatives. Relatives are defined as any persons "related to the adopted person by blood ... or by marriage". The Register is in two parts, and the Registrar's duty is to record the names of relatives and adopted people, and on receipt of a request from an adopted person who has registered, to send to them the names and contact addresses of any relatives.

Despite pressure for greater openness the Register regrettably operates only to transmit information to adopted persons in respect of their relatives. Those seeking to trace someone who was adopted are therefore entirely dependent on the adoptee to initiate the exchange of information. The Adoption Law Review, during the consultation process recommended that:

...where a birthparent or relative is proposing to contact an adult adopted person whose current address is known (or can easily be acquired) by the adoption agency which originally arranged the adoption, the agency should have the power (but not a duty) to contact the adopted person... to ask whether he or she would agree to identifying information being passed on to the parent or relative. Where an adopted person cannot easily be contacted, agencies should have the power to give identifying information about that person to a bona fide and responsible tracing agency, which could find out whether the adopted person would welcome contact.

(1992, pp. 62-63, para. 31.7)

The creation of powers rather than duties in respect of the role of agencies in helping birth family members to trace their relatives is, of course, significant. It will leave scope for great variation between agencies, in which agency ethos and philosophy will be critical.

Contact conditions prior to the Children Act

Since the passing of the first adoption legislation in 1926, there has always been a power in law for courts to impose terms and conditions on adoption orders (section 4). Section 12(6) of the Adoption Act 1976 replicating, the wording of the 1926 Act, indicates that a court may impose such "terms and conditions" as it "thinks fit" when making an adoption order.

There is, however, no indication that either the Houghton Committee (1972) or the legislators in 1976 intended that section 12 be used to facilitate continuing contact between parties to adoption, though a number of cases, which will be discussed later, have now established that this is possible.

The Children Act 1989 has brought potentially significant changes to adoption in terms of contact, primarily because proceedings in adoption are family proceedings within the meaning of the Children Act. This means that orders which can be made under the Children Act may also be made in adoption. Thus, in addition to the general power in section 12(6), the court may now, if it wishes, make a section 8 contact order in adoption. Since an adoption order operates to extinguish any other order (section12(3)), technically this order would have to be made *after* the adoption order.

Freeing orders

Freeing orders are a procedure whereby parents relinquish all of their parental responsibility prior to a full adoption hearing. Unless the child concerned is in care, at least one parent must consent to the application for an order. This application can only be made by an adoption agency. The court is under a duty to establish either that both parents willingly consent without reservation to the making of an adoption order, or, where the child is in care, and parents do not consent, their consent must be dispensed with.

When the Houghton Committee first envisaged procedures for freeing for adoption (1970, pp. 53-55) they had primarily in mind circumstances where parents wished to "free" themselves of further responsibility for a child who was to be relinquished for adoption, given the delay that was common before matters were brought to court. The provisions relating to freeing were introduced in the Children Act 1975, and subsequently incorporated into the 1976 Adoption Act when it was implemented in 1988. There was some concern, however, with the plight of children adrift in long-term care, and for this reason the final report of the Houghton Committee (1972, p. 64, para. 225) recommended, and later the legislation applied, the same general provisions concerning the dispensation of parental consent where children were in care as applied in adoption orders in section 16(2). These include dispensation on the grounds that a parent's consent has been withheld unreasonably (16(2)(b)). The significant difference in freeing provisions prior to the Children Act was that there was no power for the court, as existed in adoption under section 12(6), to attach any conditions to a freeing order.

The Children Act 1989 amended the wording of the 1976 Adoption Act, so that the term "parental rights and duties" has become "parental responsibility". It now states that on the making of a freeing order "parental responsibility is given to" the adoption agency. The effect of this is to extinguish any parental responsibility of a parent or guardian (section 12(3)) including any rights to contact. With the Children Act, however, the possibility has been created for continuing contact, through a contact order, made in conjunction with the freeing order.

Revocations of freeing orders
The freeing order permits the agency a twelve-month period during which, if a child is not already placed with prospective adopters, they may make such a placement, and parental consent to the granting of an adoption order is no longer necessary. Neither may parents contest the granting of an adoption order.

Despite, therefore, any opposition of parents or guardians, the sole consideration of the court becomes the decision about whether the particular proposed adoption would best serve the child's interests.

There is provision in the legislation for an application, as of right, by a parent or guardian for revocation of a freeing order (section 20). This right applies when a period of a year has elapsed without the making of an adoption order, and where the child is not living with a "person with whom he has been placed for adoption". This right to apply for revocation does not exist, however, for parents who made a declaration under section 18(6) of the Act to say that they no longer wished to be involved in questions concerning the adoption.

Revocations, however, have been rare it would seem (Lowe *et al*, 1991). With the lapse of contact for well over a year by the time an application is likely to be heard, there is an inevitable withering of any links that previously existed between a child and their original family. This weakening of links, where the revocation is opposed by the agency, is likely to form an important part of the basis for their argument against parents or guardians resuming parental responsibility. The resultant injustice to original families is obvious. The matter no longer rests solely on their ability effectively to resume parenting, and their case is unjustifiably weakened by the absence of continuing contact, which it has been quite beyond their powers to influence. Another injustice which results from freeing procedures as they currently exist is their failure to allow those other than parents to apply for their revocation.

The research (Lowe *et al*, 1991) indicates that in 67 per cent of freeing applications there is not parental consent, though only 22 per cent of applications are ultimately contested in the courts. Those who do not consent but fail to pursue the matter in the courts are presumably unhappy with the application but lack the will, assertiveness or resources to contest it. It is a highly unsatisfactory situation that in only one third of cases where parents are unhappy with the freeing application is the matter fully heard in court. Perhaps solicitors are advising parents of the bleakness of their prospects in successfully contesting the application since in only a tiny minority of cases do families successfully oppose freeing applications (Lowe *et al*, 1991).

Under the Children Act freeing procedures have become family proceedings, so that orders available to the court in family proceedings may be made in conjunction with freeing applications. This means that courts may now make section 8 contact orders when freeing orders have been granted. Technically, as with adoption orders, these would need to be made *after* the freeing order, since the effect of a freeing order is to extinguish any other order.

Contact orders in adoption and freeing

The Children Act offers the court what has been described as a "menu" model for making orders. Once a matter is before the court it may make whatever orders it believes will assist its overriding duty in section 1(1) of the Act to ensure that the "child's welfare" is achieved above all else. Thus where an adoption or freeing application is before the court it could use its discretion to make a contact order in respect of the child or young person. Before the Children Act only parents could apply for access (as it was then known) to a child in compulsory care. Section 10 of the Children Act specifies that any person (which would include also the child) may apply for a contact order. Some are entitled to do so; some must seek the leave of the court. This means that anyone with a meaningful relationship with a child could be granted a contact order, so the Act offers a broader definition of family than former legislation.

This expanded view of what family is has particular significance in adoption. Adoption legislation has always been founded on a belief in the desirability of heterosexually married couples as adoptive parents. The Adoption Law Review (1992, p. 49 para. 26.11) still recommends that only married couples be permitted to adopt (as a couple), and when the junior minister launched the Review on 19 October 1992 he made it clear that single adopters were not considered suitable parents in most circumstances, the sole exception being where a child was severely disabled (*The Guardian* 20/10/1992). The White

Paper on adoption, *Adoption: The Future,* while acknowledging that the law needs to reflect the full range of relationships between children and adults, states quite clearly that there must be "a strong presumption in favour of adoption by married couples" (1993, p. 9, para. 4.37).

Where an adoption order has been granted, however, the category of persons *entitled* to apply *excludes* parents and others with parental responsibility, since, according to the legal fiction upon which adoption is based, they are now *strangers* to their child. The same is almost certainly true in freeing (though this has not yet clearly been established by the courts), since, though in freeing parental responsibility is given to an agency (compared with the adopting parents under an adoption order), the responsibilities of parents and those with parental responsibility are still "extinguished".

A related but different issue is the granting of leave to former parents and relatives to apply for contact when such an application is not contemporaneous with the making of an adoption order. There has only been one reported decision of the courts in such an application to date (*Re S*, (A Minor) Contact Order, *The Times*, 8/3/1993), and this decision suggests that there ought to have been a significant change in circumstances before such leave is likely to be granted.

Contact and the welfare test
There is a confusion about the granting of contact orders in adoption which will need resolution in any new adoption legislation. The test which the court must apply in the granting of an adoption or a freeing order is that contained in section 6 of the 1976 Adoption Act. This enjoins both agencies and courts to ensure "first consideration being given ... to the welfare of the child throughout his childhood ...". This means that the court when considering both adoption and contact orders will be applying two somewhat different welfare tests in relation to a child, namely first consideration in respect of the adoption order, and paramount consideration in respect of the contact order. Where contact orders are concerned, the courts must also follow the detailed guidance available in the form of the "welfare

checklist" in section 1 of the Children Act 1989. It is likely that consideration will be given to incorporating a revised version of this checklist when adoption law is reformed. This would be likely to include paramountcy as the welfare principle in adoption except in circumstances where consideration is being given to the dispensation of parental consent.

In a Court of Appeal case in 1977, Simon LJ ([1977], AC 602) described the difference between paramountcy, which since 1925 had applied in custody and guardianship procedures, and first consideration. Paramountcy gave a status to the welfare of the child such that it was "preponderant" over *all* others, whilst first consideration meant outweighing (singly) any other consideration. It is a fine but none the less significant distinction.

The Houghton Committee (p. 61, para. 212) opted for the "first consideration" test in adoption because in their view "if the child's welfare were declared to be paramount the test of whether the mother was withholding consent unreasonably could not remain". In other words, they took the view that the introduction of a paramountcy test would render the withholding of consent an irrelevance. Thus if consideration was to be given only to children's interests to the exclusion of all others, neither parental consent nor any other consideration could be weighed in the scales with the welfare of the child. Based on their view of the separability of interests the Committee regarded (p. 62, para. 216) the making of an adoption order in contested proceedings as a matter of such gravity in terms of the consequences for the "mother" that it was essential for the law to "recognise that there are a number of interests to be considered and put the interests of the child first among them".

The idea in law of the ready separability of individual welfare interests seems at odds with the realities of social life. A more reasonable starting point might be that parental and family wishes concerning the adoption of their child are inextricably bound up with the child's ultimate welfare to such a degree that the issue of consent can not be distinguished from considerations of welfare, including the relationship with the original family.

This, interestingly, is a view which finds considerable support in the Government's consultative document of 1985 which preceded the Children Act White Paper:

A distinction is often drawn between the interests of children and those of their parents. In the majority of families, including those who are for one reason or another in need of social services, this distinction does not exist.

(p. 4, para. 2.8)

It should also be noted that while adoption legislation requires courts and agencies to give consideration to the welfare of children only throughout "his childhood" (section 6), the Children Act's welfare principle is capable of a "whole of life" interpretation. Were we to take a whole of life view of the best interests of children, we should have to consider available knowledge about adult adoptees and contact. There is evidence that the maintenance of links throughout childhood may well have been something that many adoptees would, given the opportunity of being heard at the time, have wished for.

We know that over 33,000 adoptees (DOH, *Discussion Paper 1*, 1990, p. 48) had taken advantage of section 51 of the Adoption Act by 1990. This, however, is no indication of the numbers who wish or seek such information but do not use the provisions of the Act. In countries like Australia (notably the State of Victoria) and New Zealand, where access to birth records information has been fully and carefully advertised, including television advertising, the take up of access provisions by adoptees has been much higher. In New Zealand it has been estimated (Griffith, 1991, p. 155) that in a five-year period from the implementation of new legislation, 40 per cent of adoptees who were adopted by strangers used the birth records provisions of the Adult Adoption Information Act 1985. Based on a revision in 1992 of an estimate originally made in 1987 (Hodgkins, 1992), it is estimated that over the whole of life the number of adoptees adopted by strangers in England and Wales likely to search their origins is 64 per cent, with the ratio of men to women being two to one.

Contact and the judiciary

There have been few adoption orders with contact despite the general powers of the courts since 1926 to attach to adoption orders whatever terms and conditions they deem appropriate. However, the power to make an order with a condition of contact was clearly established prior to the Children Act 1989. In *Re M* ([1986] 1 FLR 51) the Court of Appeal, whilst supporting the traditional judicial view that continuing contact after adoption was generally undesirable, was clear that it was within the power of the court to make a condition as to access [contact]. At the same time the court emphasised its view that to force contact against the wishes of adopting parents would be very undesirable.

In an important more recent case the House of Lords (*Re C* [1989], AC 1) overturned the decision of the Court of Appeal that it did not have jurisdiction to make an adoption order in respect of a ward of court which would attach a condition for continuing access between her and her brother. Reviewing the decisions in other cases the court concluded that it was appropriate *normally* for the judiciary to exclude the idea of continuing access in adoption, but that nonetheless *each case* must be considered on its individual circumstances. The court also emphasised that, where access with members of the original family was opposed by adopting parents, conditions concerning contact should be imposed only in very rare circumstances. The court additionally stated that should the adopting parents fail to comply with the order they could face committal for contempt.

It is hard to imagine circumstances in which any enforcement of a contact order in adoption may not potentially have harmful consequences for children. If a view is taken that the best interests of a child will be served by the continuation of contact, it would seem to be a breach of the welfare duty placed on agencies and courts under section 6 of the Adoption Act 1976 to make a placement with adopting parents where such contact is potentially possible only through the enforcement of an order. In these instances the agency should be seeking permanent placements other than by adoption, or placements with adopters who whole-heartedly recognise the value of contact. As Fratter's research (1989) indicates, such adopters can be found where agencies themselves are committed to the principle of contact.

In contrast to the few situations where conditions of contact have been made with adoption orders, there have been many instances where the court is aware of plans for contact, (see for example *Re W* [1988], 1 FLR 175) but has been happy for this to be negotiated between the parties themselves.

In a recent case in the High Court (*Re M and J (Minors)* [1992], not yet reported) where a brother and sister were wards of court, an application by the local authority for leave to place the children for adoption and to terminate the contact with their parents (both of whom suffered mental ill health) was declined. It was accepted by the parents that they were not able effectively to parent their children. They wished, however, to maintain contact with them and had been seeing the children, aged two and four years, on a weekly basis. The local authority argued that the task of placing the children together was difficult in itself and that the continuation of contact would compound this difficulty. They also argued that the contact there had been was not of great importance to the children.

The judge disagreed that the contact was unimportant, despite the fact that the children were young and had spent little time in parental care. She came to the view that a permanent placement by way of foster care could in these circumstances more easily be found. Accordingly she did not give leave to place for adoption and ordered that contact continue on a twice weekly basis while a permanent family was sought, and that when the children were permanently placed contact should be maintained twice a month. On appeal this decision stood except that the frequency of contact was reduced to once a fortnight.

Such decisions are likely to be rare in the immediate future. A new form of permanent care, however, such as *inter vivos* guardianship[1] might be seen by the courts as an acceptable alternative to adoption in circumstances where the maintenance of contact was regarded as important.

Law and practice
Social Work practice and the law often exist in uneasy relationship. Research has shown that new legislation may do little to influence prevailing practice (Ryburn, 1991b). A case in point is the *Code of Practice on Access to Children in Care*, introduced by the Secretary of State pursuant to section 12c (3) of the Child Care Act 1980. The research of Millham and his colleagues (1989) indicated very clearly that many practitioners were quite unaware of its existence, families were not advised of the rights that it gave them, and many local authorities failed to establish the appeals procedures that they were required to set up under its terms. The failure of the *Code of Practice* demonstrates that it takes more than a change in the legal framework to influence practice. What is necessary is to win the hearts and minds of practitioners.

New Zealand is widely regarded as leading western adoption practice with respect to openness (Mullender, 1990). Though there was reform of the law in 1985 which restored to adults in adoption rights to information, the primary legislation is still that of 1955, introduced at a time when the world-wide trend in western practice favoured secrecy (Griffith, 1981, p. 45). It gives no encouragement to open practice and there is, for example, no provision for the attachment of conditions to the making of adoption orders.

Like the legislation here, however, it does not prohibit parties, on the basis of negotiated agreement, choosing to remain in contact with each other after an adoption. Goodwill-based agreements for continuing contact after adoption have become almost universal in New Zealand over the past two decades. They

---

[1] This has been recommended in the Law Review Consultation Document (1992, p.15, para. 6.5), and the White Paper (1993, p.13, para. 5.24).

have been accompanied by the opening of adoptions that were originally closed, and the active tracing of birth relatives, which began long before the law made this easier. Perhaps it is the lack of legislative provision for openness which has paradoxically encouraged its practice!

Openness in New Zealand works because it has built steadily on the experiences of its adoption consumers and the commitment of practitioners. Though the law has not been an irrelevance, neither has its role been critical.

In New Zealand, Australia and the United States, where there has been a move to more open practice, consumer groups have often played a crucial role. Here too, in the United Kingdom, with the development of post-adoption services shaped by experiences of those who are parties to adoption and their expressed needs (see for example Howe, 1990) and the united voice of consumer groups such as NORCAP (National Organisation for Counselling of Adopted People), The Natural Parents Support Group, PPIAS (Parent-to-Parent Information on Adoption Services), The United Kingdom Grandparents Federation, and ADOPT (in Northern Ireland), there is growing pressure for more informed and flexible practice. The call for practice that is more responsive and less professionally led will continue slowly to roll back the barriers of secrecy - but is this sufficient to ensure open models of placement and practice?

Changes in practice to facilitate openness
There are many changes in practice that could be accomplished without change to the law; indeed even were the law to change the realisation of openness may still fundamentally depend on practitioners.

There is nothing to prevent agencies developing models for assessment in adoption which are founded on the principles of openness and participation rather than professional infallibility (see Howell and Ryburn, 1987; Ryburn, 1991a; Stevenson,

1991). There is no reason not to involve birth parents or other relatives in the selection of families for their children.[2]

There has never been anything to prevent agencies offering a "post box" service to those who wish to remain in contact via an intermediary after adoption. There is no prohibition against people who wish to, remaining in contact on whatever basis they choose following an adoption, and research like that of Fratter's, (1991) shows that this can and does happen in the United Kingdom. There is now nothing to prevent parties to adoption asking, in all their interests, if they wish to formalise an agreement, for a contact order to be made following the adoption order. This could have some parallels with the negotiated agreements that have been proposed in Western Australia (van Keppel, 1991).

Changes in the law to facilitate openness
There *is* a need for change in the law if we are to retain adoption. The law, as Jane Rowe wrote of the Children Bill in 1989, can support social workers in achieving good practice, and can offer a mandate to good practice in the face of institutional and bureaucratic inertia and opposition.

Changes that would be helpful include the repeal of the freeing provisions which are manifestly unjust and do not give full consideration to each child's welfare. They constitute in effect *de facto* adoption orders, at a mid-point in the adoption process, and mean that full and proper consideration of all the circumstances is not given at the final hearing. It seems likely following consultation on the adoption White Paper that freeing will indeed be abolished, though the recommendation for a new form of order called a placement order (spelled out in the Adoption Law Review Consultation Document, p. 23, para. 15.1) may in effect be little other than freeing in a different guise.

---

[2] This is something which the Adoption Law Review indicates is already beginning to happen (*Paper 1*, 1990, p. 60, para. 100).

The Consultation Document (1992, p. 18, paras. 7.5-7.6) recommends a checklist in relation to the welfare of the child which is commensurate with the checklist in section 1(3) of the Children Act 1989, with the addition of a duty to consider the importance for a child of contact with all those important to him or her, and whether the continuation of significant links would be possible following the granting of an adoption order. Such a checklist would be a major step forward in beginning to accord the importance to the maintenance of contact that is justified by a considerable body of research (see below chapter four).

The lack of evidence in research (see below chapter four) to support the idea that permanence for children and young people is necessarily best achieved by adoption could be given recognition in another suggestion in the White Paper (p. 13, paras. 5.23-5.27) which is for the introduction of *inter vivos* guardianship. This guardianship would in effect grant to a carer all the responsibilities of a parent with the exception of the right to consent to adoption or to change a child's surname. Perhaps more than any other legal provision this could encourage more open practice in the permanent placement of children. It would do so by beginning to challenge the view identified as least as long ago as 1984 in the Short Report, (p. 78) that there was an undesirable perception of a hierarchy of permanent placement options for children amongst professionals in which adoption was at the pinnacle. The effect on openness of such a hierarchy is obvious, and to challenge it is to begin to create the preconditions for more open practice.

Though it has not been suggested in the White Paper, the possibility should be considered of restoring to birth parents the right that existed to them before the granting of an adoption order, to apply without leave for a contact order. There would still be available to the court under section 91 of the Children Act a power to prevent any named person applying for an order without leave, but at least there would then be the creation of a presumption of contact between birth parents and their children which was consistent in all child care proceedings, including adoption.

One of the recommendations of the Law Review (1992, p. 16, para. 7.2) is that adoption should be recognised as a life-long phenomenon, and that a 'whole of life approach' by the courts is therefore necessary. If the life-long nature of adoption is to be fully recognised then this cannot be done without giving greater weighting to the Review's recommendations for much wider rights to identifying information for all parties in adoption, (1992, pp. 62-3, para. 31.7). Studies in relation to reunions in adoption (see for example Rockel and Ryburn, p. 79) indicate that a whole range of birth relatives may become important in the lives of adult adoptees. The recommendation that there be a power rather than a duty on local authorities to help birth relatives to find adult adoptees seems significantly inadequate and even this limited recognition of the needs of birth relatives finds no apparent support in the 1993 adoption White Paper.

Finally, perhaps the most helpful change in adoption law would be to make explicit a general principle of the Children Act, that children ought where ever possible to be parented within the networks of their own families. Many children who are in State care or have been adopted could have been restored to their families (Trent, 1989). As the Short Report (1984) so rightly pointed out, the need for public child care provision could be greatly reduced, with advantage to all, if the weight of resources shifted from substitute to original families. The legislation could require that no order be made for the substitute care of any child until a planning meeting involving all significant people in a child's family network had failed to suggest a suitable in-family placement.

Conclusion
Open practice in adoption is best achieved through a partnership between law and practice. Openness should not be viewed as radical or untried. There is ample research and practice to support it (see below chapter four). Current adoption legislation, and much adoption practice which fails to take sufficient account of the importance of original family links for all children, can more properly be seen as out of step with the Children Act.

2 Identity formation

Introduction

The achievement of a satisfying personal identity, which can broadly be defined as a sense of psychosocial well-being (Erikson, 1959), is an issue of major importance in the literature on human development. In addition much child care planning and decision-making is informed by theoretical ideas about healthy identity formation. Adoption is widely regarded as creating for all parties inherently contradictory relationships that are likely to increase the difficulties of identity formation (see for example Schoenberg, 1974). Ideas about the best way to achieve a clear and positive sense of personal identity in adoption have often been influential in the formulation of policy and in shaping practice, and have informed too much of the debate about openness and secrecy.

It has long been assumed, because adoption represents a clearly recognisable bridge between nurture and nature, that issues in relation to the development of personality and behavioural characteristics will here be at their most clear. This particular interest in adoption as the ideal field for research and inquiry into the relative influence of genetic and environmental factors began with Richardson in 1913 and it has since provided the impetus for countless research studies. Identity formation, however, is one aspect of human development where comparative research between adopted and non-adopted populations has been relatively slight, though there has been a considerable body of research into identity formation itself.

In the absence of any substantial body of research relating directly to identity formation in adoption it is important to understand the profile of identity research in order to assess its usefulness for the adoption field and to locate identity issues in adoption in context. This chapter first reviews mainstream identity theory and research and considers their application and usefulness in the adoption field. Alternative perspectives are discussed and a distinction is drawn between identity achievement and the measure of satisfaction and happiness that this identity brings. The following chapter which considers more specifically aspects of identity in adoption, draws on the accounts of parties to adoption to highlight the particular identity issues adoptive status may bring.

The concept of personal identity

The idea of personal identity, a sense of self, has been a consistent theme in Western culture, including religion, over the centuries. There are two interrelated ideas associated with the traditional concept of identity. The first concerns its discovery and realisation "know thyself"; the second, its capacity to serve as a benchmark for charting action and behaviour in the future: "to thine own self be true".

During this century as the idea of identity has become an important focus for theoretical consideration and research two distinct strands have developed. Mainstream theory and research has followed in the Aristotelian tradition and has principally been led by psychologists from North America. The alternative positions and views have been contributed by feminist and cross-cultural perspectives, and different frameworks for analysis, including social constructionist and systemic perspectives, as well, more recently, as the deconstructionism of Jacques Derrida (1974, 1978, 1984).

The North American tradition

Erik Erikson (1956, 1959, 1968, 1980) is widely regarded as the key figure in modern identity theory. Erikson (1968) offered a broad definition of identity (the achievement of which he described as the key developmental task of adolescence) when he wrote:

The wholeness to be achieved at this stage [adolescence] I have called a sense of inner identity. The young person, in order to experience wholeness, must feel a progressive continuity between that which he has come to be during the long years of childhood and that which he promises to become in the anticipated future; between that which he conceives himself to be and that which he perceives others to see in him and to expect of him. Individually speaking identity includes but is more than, the sum of all successive identifications of those earlier years when the child wanted to be, and was often forced to become, like the person he depended on. Identity is a unique product, which now meets a crisis to be solved only in new identifications with age mates and with figures outside the family.

(p. 87)

Though Erikson's definition of identity is broad he does define certain key aspects of identity. These are specific foci around which all of us, he maintains, develop to a greater or lesser extent a reflective self-awareness. They centre on philosophy of life, ideology (including such things as political and religious beliefs), vocation, ethnicity, culture, nationality, gender, sexuality, and the relationship that each of us has with what Erikson (1968, p. 42) calls an "all-inclusive" human identity.

Writing in 1980 Erikson describes how each of us constructs a sense of identity in relation to our given characteristics, through the process of making decisions and electing particular courses of action within our social environments. This process is described by Erikson in terms of a personal crisis. It leads (1959, p. 74) to "a more final self-definition, to irreversible role patterns, and thus to commitments 'for Life'". The development of the resultant sense of personal identity can give a feeling of psychological and social welfare and "of being at home in one's body, a sense of knowing where one is going" (p. 127), and (1956, p. 74) "an inner assuredness of anticipated recognition from those who count". Erikson also rates highly in this process the development of a sense of inner coherence which is continuous over time, for this creates, he claims, our necessary sense of connectedness to the outside world. The ability of each of us to develop a sense of identity is essential to a capacity to meet with and manage situations of crisis and difficulty in the future (Erikson, 1968). The achievement of personal identity, in Erikson's theoretical formulation, is assumed to have a universal importance in the West that transcends the boundaries of culture and class and the distinctiveness that something like the status of adoption brings with it.

The key problem, from a research perspective, with the Eriksonian theory of identity development has been the challenge presented by its all encompassing nature. James Marcia (1966, 1980) has played an influential role in operationalising the concept of identity for research purposes. Marcia developed a paradigm representing four different identity statuses and developed an instrument, the Identity Status Interview, for their assessment. The statuses are seen to result from the reflexive interaction of the process of identity formation with individual personality characteristics. The status achieved becomes the key determinant of how the world is viewed.

These statuses exist in relation to two particular dimensions, *exploration* and *commitment.* Exploration ("know thyself") describes the active quest necessary in order to acquire self-knowledge in aspects of identity such as religious beliefs, attitudes to work or choice of vocation. Commitment ("to thine own self be true") is the process of making sure and firm decisions in these areas, and acting to implement them appropriately.

At the least developed level is the status of *identity diffusion,* which is characterised by lack of internal goals and values that are consistent. Those in identity diffusion are likely, Marcia claims (1966, 1980), always to assume the easiest course of action; it is a status largely lacking both exploration and commitment. A different status is that of *identity foreclosure*, which represents a high level of commitment to certain principles, values and ways of interacting, with no or little consideration of alternatives. *Moratorium* represents a more developed status in which there is intense searching aimed to achieve identity vocationally, philosophically and in relationships, but with the absence of any sense of resolution of this concerted exploration. The final status in Marcia's typology is that of *identity achievement.*

Identity achievement represents the establishment, for Marcia, of a clear sense of self through the possession of internally consistent principles, values and philosophy and the commitment and ability to use these critically as a guide for conduct and relationships in the social world. Identity achievement is the outgrowth of the exploration that occurs during moratorium. Marcia (1980, p. 161) writes that "There are *both* healthy and pathological aspects of each of the styles, save perhaps the Identity Achiever status". Development can occur progressively from one status to another.

Much research on identity formation (see for example the review by Waterman, 1982) has viewed it as a way to understand individual behaviour in our environment. The sorts of statuses identified by Marcia have been regarded as a means of understanding feelings and cognition, social relationships and behaviour. To Marcia's fourth status, Waterman (1990) has added an extra dimension, which he calls "personal expressiveness". The missing element he identifies in Marcia's identity achievement status is the sense to which any action is "personally expressive", in other words the extent to which it is accompanied by a special and intense feeling of fitting appropriately with what a person believes exemplifies who they truly are or what they really intended to do.

Research within the tradition established by Erikson has been considerable, and has often involved the use of Marcia's (1966, 1980) Identity Status Interview (ISI). It has customarily sought to establish the relationship between different identity statuses and aspects of successful social and psychological functioning.

One of the most researched areas has been the relationship between identity and mental health. In this area studies have shown fairly consistently that those who have attained the status of identity achievement have less reported mental and emotional disturbance and ill health (see for example Howard and Kubis, 1964; Marcia, 1967; Stark and Traxler, 1974). The relationship between feelings of happiness, acceptance of self, self-esteem and identity formation has also been the subject of considerable research. Research again establishes a relationship between the achievement of a clear sense of personal identity and high levels of self-acceptance and esteem, but principally for men (see for example Adams *et al*, 1979, Read *et al*, 1984).

Other research, using Laurence Kohlberg's (1964) different stages of moral reasoning and development, has shown a consistent relationship between higher levels on the Kohlberg scale and identity achievement (see for example Hult, 1979; Rowe and Marcia, 1980). Rothman (1984) and others have found those with higher levels of identity formation conduct their lives with a greater sense of purpose. Adams and Shea (1979), amongst others, have also found heightened senses of self-responsibility and control in this same group.

A shortcoming of this body of research is that it has nearly all tended to be cross-sectional rather than longitudinal, a significant failing in a model that subscribes in general to the idea of a progressive development in identity formation over the life-span. The research is also heavily weighted towards self-report as a method of data collection, and although it is largely informed by the same theoretical constructs, comparable measures have often not been employed.

Application in adoption
The Eriksonian formulation of self-identity, and the framework developed to research it, have had little rigorous application in the adoption field. This is surprising since adoption has continued to provide a fertile field for those interested in the nature-nurture debate (see for example Plomin and DeFries, 1985).

The explanation for the lack of research relates probably to the difficulties of carrying it out, rather than to a lack of interest in making comparisons. Clinical populations were the primary source for samples of adoptees in earlier studies (see for example Offord *et al*, 1969; Schechter *et al*, 1964; Toussieng, 1962). There was, however, a recognition in the early 1970s that there is limited *general* value in comparative studies where samples derive from clinical populations. General population samples, however, need to be very large, as they were for example in the National Child Development study (Seglow *et al*, 1972), in order to yield enough adoptees. Neither are adoption agencies necessarily a useful source of adoptees for research purposes as often they tend to lose contact soon after adoption; nor do such self-selected samples meet all the criteria for representative sampling and unless a sample can be drawn from a range of agencies there are further problems of potential bias.

Most of the research in adoption that follows the Eriksonian model has tended to indicate no important difference in identity achievement between those who are and those who are not adopted. Two studies are worth mentioning in particular. Norvell and Guy (1977), comparing non-clinical samples of 38 adoptees and 38 non-adoptees, found that the adoption group scored slightly higher mean scores on the Berger Self-Concept scale. They concluded that adoptive status did not pose any particular dimensions of difficulty, and drew the conclusion that the specifics of the relationships between parents and children were the most significant factors in identity formation.

Stein and Hoopes (1985) studied a non-clinical sample of 50 adopted and 41 non-adopted young people aged 15 to 18. Their sample was part of the major Delaware Family Study. They used a semi-structured interview and two other identity measures, the Offer Self-Image Questionnaire (Offer, 1973), and the Tan Ego Identity Scale (Tan *et al*, 1977). They discovered no significant differences between the two groups in terms of identity formation.

The trouble, however, with the general measures such as Marcia's ISI, that are based on Eriksonian theory, is that they do not raise in sufficient detail the sorts of issues and questions that would be likely to elicit from adoptees information concerning the particular identity difficulties *in adoption* that have been reported in other studies (see for example Baran *et al*, 1975; Triseliotis, 1973; Triseliotis and Russell, 1984; Rockel and Ryburn, 1988). In other words whether adoptees obtain high or low scores on these measures, the relationship of the resultant score to the subject's adoptive status is not investigated and established in any way.

Research based on Eriksonian formulations of identity achievement which compares adopted and non-adopted groups raises at best the question of the inter-relationship between the different components of self-identity. It does not offer any substantive commentary on the absence or otherwise of significant differences in identity achievement between adoptees and others. Nor does it do anything to explain whether difficulties in identity formation are at all a factor in the apparent over-representation of a variety of behavioural and psychological problems amongst adopted children (adopted from infancy and early childhood) in studies of clinical populations (see for example Deutsch *et al*, 1982; Howe and Hinings, 1987; Humphrey and Ounsted, 1963), and, to a lesser extent, in community based-samples (see for example Brodzinsky *et al*, 1984; Brodzinsky *et al*, 1987; Hoopes, 1982; Raynor, 1980).

In mainstream North American, and to a lesser extent European psychology, the Eriksonian model has reigned supreme and largely indifferent to an avalanche of direct and implied criticism from various quarters. It is important to summarise some of this criticism for it points us to more useful ways of looking at identity achievement for those who are adopted.

Alternative views
Feminists
Feminists have been critical of the theory for its predominant reliance on research by men about men and its extrapolation from these findings to women (see for example Gilligan, 1982). They also point out that in the few studies that involve women there tend to be different findings compared with men (see for example Marcia and Friedman, 1970; Schenkel and Marcia, 1972). Thus women rated as identity achievers have very low ratings on self-esteem, unlike their male counterparts, (Marcia and Friedman, 1970). This indicates a failure of the model to address the issue of the unacceptability for women of being assertive in a male dominated social order, and it throws into doubt its usefulness for intra-gender studies.

Cultural relevance

Cross-cultural studies have shown the model to be strongly North American in its bias (see for example Shweder and Bourne, 1982), and its prevailing emphasis is further narrowed by its predominantly white and (as has been noted) male bias. Indeed at least one study (Schiedal and Marcia, 1985) shows a clear relationship between the attainment of identity and high levels of "masculinity".

Another criticism that can be made of the social view that the model encompasses is that its essential emphasis on progression through a hierarchy of levels of attainment depends on the notion of "identity failures", against whom achievers can be compared. It is but a small step to begin to view such "failures" in moral terms.

Systemic thinking and constructionism

The alternative framework for identity which is afforded by systemic thinking disputes the very idea of the distinct entities upon which it is based. The world for systemic theorists is viewed in relational terms, where observers are always part of what they observe. It is a world in which there are no final closures, but rather only the distinctions that observers make (see for example Bateson, 1972; Anderson and Goolishian, 1987; Maturana and Varela, 1987).

Social constructionist thinking draws originally on the work of Mead (1934), pre-dating the work of Erikson by almost twenty years. He proposed that identity was primarily shaped by social interaction rather than intra-psychic processes. His ideas have subsequently been influential for social constructionists, who take issue with the dominant belief, in identity theory and research, of a "true self" awaiting realisation. Constructionists argue that research which centres on a belief in immanent qualities which, through the interplay of exploration, choice and commitment, come together to constitute identity, is founded on premises which cannot be sustained. They maintain that personality characteristics, indeed the very idea of self and identity are socially and historically constructed, and that these are not phenomena that can be found to occur naturally. They would take issue therefore with Erikson's idea of a normative crisis from which stems discovery, choice and commitment since, as early constructionists Berger and Luckmann (1967) write, so many are never permitted an alternative to the questions about identity:

*... the socially predefined answer is massively real subjectively and consistently confirmed in all significant social interaction. This by no means implies that the individual is happy with his identity. It was probably never very agreeable to be a peasant, for instance. To be a peasant entailed problems of all sorts ... It did **not** entail the problem of identity. One was a miserable, perhaps even rebellious peasant. But one **was** a peasant.*

(p. 184)

Deconstructionism

Following from the work of Derrida, a further major challenge is implied in relation to the Eriksonian idea of identity. Erikson's model and the research based on it place the highest value on the resolution of opposites, on wholeness and integration. Deconstructionists challenge the very notion that a process, like that of identity formation, is bounded by "points of origin or conclusion" (Derrida, 1978 p. 226). Derrida argues for a world in which "the punctual simplicity of the classical subject is not to be found" (1978, p. 227). It is a world in which there is no hierarchy of meaning and thus no integrative force intent on forging personal identity to the exclusion of other influences.

Of all the points of departure, so far as adoption is concerned, from the theoretical framework that bounds Eriksonian identity theory, the most significant are perhaps those of the feminists and the social constructionists. The issue fundamentally is not whether there is *identity diffusion* or *identity achievement*, it is about the degree of "happiness" that exists with whatever that sense of identity is. To have attained Marcia's (1966, 1980) identity achievement status is neither to imply nor to deny happiness with that identity. If we accept Berger and Luckmann's contention (1967), it would be perfectly possible for adoptees to score highly on identity achievement or to show no differences overall in comparison with their non adopted peers in terms of identity formation, yet still to be unhappy with this identity. The distinction between clarity of identity and happiness with identity is a critical one. In so far as the identity achievement measures are reliable, this surely, as Gilligan (1982) suggests, is the only reasonable explanation for high identity achievers who are women (in comparison with male counterparts) scoring low ratings on self-esteem. To achieve, as a woman, clarity of vision about identity in a social world which is seen to be predicated on male norms and values may do little to raise self-esteem.

Beyond the major criticisms that can be made of the premises upon which Eriksonian theory is founded, it does not discriminate between what Baumeister in his analysis of self-definition (1986), defines as "assigned" rather than "chosen" elements of identity, and nor does it distinguish highly visible (for example ethnicity) and largely invisible (for example adoption) components of assigned identity. It further fails to seek to understand these in terms of reflexive relationships in which each interacts with, and mediates the other. Finally, if identity formation constitutes an "integration" in Eriksonian terms, the very study of discrete elements is at odds with this approach and, as has been noted, clarity of personal identity does not guarantee *happiness* with that same identity.

The Eriksonian model is at its most pernicious when applied to groups who are socially disadvantaged. It is not only that it ignores social realities, though those living in inner city deprivation certainly have little occasion to indulge themselves in a period of *moratorium* while they explore options and contemplate choices. It is a recipe for the preservation of the social status quo, since it locates the achievement of identity, social achievement in general, and by implication "failure" as well in the domain of intra-psychic processes, rather than structural inequalities and injustice.

In its application to adoption there are similar risks, since identity failures (those for example who "need to search", those who are uncertain, those who are grieving and in "identity

31

diffusion") are likely to be viewed in terms of psychological deficits. It is a model which encourages little or no consideration of adoption policy and practice as a factor in shaping identity, or of the social construction of meaning in adoption. Secrecy, (or "confidentiality" as North Americans euphemistically call it) which is still the policy at the heart of society's construction of 'best adoption practice', rather than openness, works in tandem with traditional identity theory. Their combined effect is to prevent debate reaching the domain of human rights, so that the issues for those struggling with adoption identity remain framed in terms of personal psychopathology rather than public policy. While secrecy prevails, guilt (see for example Sachdev, 1991) and a fear of discussing personal concerns may still be the experience of many who seek to come to terms with their identities in adoption.

3 Identity in adoption

Self-concept and self-esteem

If mainstream identity theory fails to yield a very useful definition for the purposes of discussion of identity in adoption, there is need for an alternative. There are twin aspects to identity. One is how we understand at a cognitive level who we are (often called self-concept). The other is how we feel about this self-understanding, which is where the term self-esteem fits in. Though we can distinguish these two key aspects of identity it is not useful to see them as discrete. They exist in a dynamic and reflexive relationship, within a social environment.

Self-concept will depend critically on the amount of information that we have about ourselves, which for those who are adopted will include the amount of information that is available concerning their original families and background. The measure of individual self-esteem that each of us achieves in relation to self-concept will be determined critically by the messages that are received or understood in our social environment. These messages offer a constant variety of perspectives concerning the information on which self-concept is built. Where self-concept is clear and accompanied by a positive self-esteem, discordant messages can be shrugged off or accommodated. It is only when messages that conflict with self-concept assume sufficient importance to challenge self-esteem that there may be problems in the achievement of a satisfying personal identity.

Challenges to identity achievement

Identity, both our concept of self, and self-esteem, the measure of positive feelings which we have concerning self-concept, are important because they determine the ways and the degree of confidence with which we enter our social world. The responses of others to us not only shape how we perceive ourselves but are also shaped by our self perceptions, since these govern to a large extent our behaviour and responses. An approach to adoption identity issues which addresses both social and personal concerns and recognises that they are inextricably linked is therefore the most useful.

Two particular kinds of discordant messages can be identified, which, if they are sufficiently powerful, are likely to alter self-concept and self-esteem. The first is messages about difference in terms of personal characteristics, including both physical and personality qualities, where such difference is either not valued or not perceived to be valued. The other is messages about being different in terms of some social status, role or attribute, where that difference is again not construed positively (Goffman's "stigma", 1963).

The fact of adoption can be seen as adding a dimension to each of these categories that broadens the range of possible negative messages that can either be received or perceived, with resultant effects on self-concept and self-esteem.

It does so in two different but inter-linked ways. First, the personal loss of genetic continuity that adoption occasions (at least in the absence of continuing contact with an original family) brings with it the loss of a reference point, a way to make sense of personal attributes, qualities and characteristics, and of many of the clues that others take for granted in the development of self-concept.

Second, the meaning and value that many societies, including our own, attribute to continuity creates more general difficulties in the acquisition of a clear and positive sense of personal identity. The social emphasis on continuity shows itself in myriad ways including a preoccupation with written and oral history, genealogy and the value of consanguineal, over social, kinship. It is also to be found in the *progression* through a 'normal' life-cycle with education records, health and employment 'histories', partnerships, self-perpetuation through procreation, and the well earned denouement of retirement. Yet current adoption practice and law, as has been noted, is now largely located in discontinuity, even if we would not subscribe entirely to its intentions as described by a High Court judge:

In general, it is the policy of the law to make the veil between past and present lives of adopted persons as opaque and impenetrable as possible, like the veil which God has placed between the living and the dead.

(Griffith, 1989, p. 46)

In a society where continuity was not valued, words such as those above would pose no great threat to the identity of adopted people. In a society, however, in which the predominant religious tradition begins "In the beginning", and stories start "Once upon a time" in a distant yet still connected past, it would be surprising if for at least some who are adopted, they are not distressing words indeed. They serve immediately to distinguish those that are adopted from the vast majority of other people. To lose connection with the past can be, in our society, to lose one's self.

It is important to acknowledge that we will never be able to establish the extent to which there are shared levels of concern or distress about particular aspects of identity within the adoption community. Very few studies offer more than a snapshot at one point in time. Very seldom do they involve the study of older people in adoption. Yet identity is an issue *for life*, and, mediated by time and changing circumstance, will not be the same tomorrow as it is today. We can therefore never be sure that those who express identity problems in adoption will continue to do so, or that those who express no such concerns may not do so at a later point in life.

The single matter on which we can be relatively sure is that when issues of continuity are to the fore, perhaps at certain stages of development, or at times of anniversary or rites of passage, then the discontinuity adoption may bring with it, or emphasise, can sometimes create or heighten identity difficulties. Yet it would be a mistake also to see the emphasis on continuity as primarily expressed in major events. As some of the accounts below testify, issues of continuity may arise in countless ways that none of us would be able to anticipate. In considering the factors that heighten identity problems we should look also to policy and practice to see whether there are changes that could make a difference.

Traditionally, when identity has been considered in relation to adoption, it has been viewed primarily in relation to adopted people (see for example McWhinnie 1967; Triseliotis, 1973). Concerns expressed by adopting parents or members of original families have tended to attract other labels. Thus the infertility of many adopters, or the loss of relinquishing parents, has frequently been constructed as a grief process (which it is) rather than in relation to the inseparably linked identity issues. The remainder of this chapter explores challenges to self-concept, self-esteem and therefore to identity formation, from the starting point of the accounts of those who are adopted. It seeks also, however, to draw out where there may be threads common to birth parents and adopting parents.

Telling and identity

When and how they learned about their being adopted, in the case of those adopted in early years, or the degree of clarity about their adoptive status, for those adopted when older, is something that can present a major challenge to existing self-concept or to the development of self-concept. It may for some adoptees become a potent source of insecurity and identity anxieties.

Even where children are told of their adoption when they are very young the sense of difference that this can create may be disturbing. This includes those with good memories of the actual experience of being told.

I was chosen. Told in a nice way ... [though] the memories of being told are good ... I didn't like it and still don't. I felt I never belonged anywhere and I never wanted to accept the fact that I was adopted. It was only a partial acceptance. They accepted it; as far as they were concerned I was their daughter and that was it.

(Picton and Bieske-Vos, 1982, p. 37)

This adult adoptee described growing up always with the knowledge of being adopted, but little substantive detail, because her adopters knew very little too:

One of the things that I switched off as a young child was allowing people to be close to me. I've always had this fear that somehow, if I did, they would be taken away, and that's fairly much influenced my life all the way through. If I've actually opened up and let somebody get close to me, I've tended to be very possessive, but more often I've kept my distance - even with my own children. I think that old fear of them being taken away is one of the shadows of adoption in my life.

(Rockel and Ryburn, 1988, p. 50)

Where the knowledge of being adopted comes later in childhood, or in adolescence, it can for some children force a major reappraisal of who they are. This 27-year-old man in Picton and Bieske-Vos's study describes being told in middle childhood:

We were sitting by the fire one night talking quietly. Father said "you are our own adopted son." I said, "I feel strange." Mother said, "You don't have to worry, you are still ours." After that moment I felt uneasy. I knew what it meant - I knew I hadn't been born to them.

(p. 39)

In our study in New Zealand (1988) we found several instances in the case of adoptions dating from the 1950s where telling about adoption was left until it was judged that an adopted person had reached adulthood. It seemed to have been seen by adopters as a sort of rite of passage, and it probably reflects advice that they may have been given at the time of adoption:

I was told officially when I was eighteen. But I can remember, looking back over my life, getting all sorts of little clues from when I was very small. I remember one scene quite well, probably before I went to school. We must have been talking and my mother said, "but you wouldn't mind if you were adopted, would you?" I burst into tears and begged her to tell me I wasn't adopted. And she said "no I wasn't".

(Rockel and Ryburn, 1988, p. 46)

Another group of adoptees recounted learning of their adoption from someone other than a parent, and the effect that this had on both their feelings about themselves and their relationships with parents could be profound:

I didn't know anything about it at all until I was about eleven and I was told in the school playground. It was devastating. I know it made me feel very insecure, because I had no idea that I was adopted, and I'd always thought of my adoptive parents as my birth parents. I lost a lot of confidence at that point.

(Rockel and Ryburn, 1988, p. 46)

Other studies have reported similar findings. In Picton and Bieske-Vos's study (1982), for example, ten of forty-eight adoptees were told of adoption by someone other than a parent.

Where we found in our study adoptees who did not learn until adulthood of being adopted, this information could become a major challenge to self-concept and self-esteem.

I was in my forties when I discovered that the people I thought were my parents were really my grandparents. It was an awful moment. I felt at first as though a big black pit had opened up in front of me, and I was standing on the edge trying not to fall in.

(Rockel and Ryburn, 1988, p. 47)

Both Triseliotis (1973) and McWhinnie (1967), as has been noted, also found that it could be devastating for adopted people to learn of their adoptions in adulthood. Perhaps most difficult can be the feeling of breach of trust that this creates in relationships with adoptive parents. This was well summed up by a thirty-year-old woman in Picton and Bieske-Vos's study who learned of adoption in her early twenties. She recounted that:

I was very bitter. It took five years before I could see my adoptive parents in a respectable light.

(p. 44)

Learning late about adoption also shatters the sense of genealogical continuity that was thought to be there, and again this is an enormous challenge to self-concept and esteem and creates the need for a complete reassessment of many significant relationships. This reappraisal was the focus of an interview with a thirty-five-year old man who described it in the following terms:

When I first learned I couldn't see anything in the same way anymore. I just felt that all these years I'd been living a lie that I hadn't known about. Others had known but not me. How could things ever be the same again.

(previously unpublished interview extract, Rockel and Ryburn, 1988)

Understanding and identity
Brodzinsky and his colleagues (1984a, 1984b) have also highlighted that it is not just the telling that is important, it is the manner of the telling. Adoption is an enormously complex idea for children to grasp. Drawing on Piagetian schema for cognitive development (Piaget, 1963) they were able to demonstrate in their research that explanations given to children concerning adoption had to be carefully matched to levels of understanding or a "cognitive dissonance" (Festinger, 1957) could result. This applied both to explanations that were too complicated and those that lacked sophistication. They concluded that until children had reached Piaget's formal operations stage they could achieve only a very limited understanding of the meaning of adoption. They also demonstrated that the process of understanding adoption continued into adolescence.

The issue of age-appropriate explanation is considered further in the chapter based on interviews with Matthew and Annabel (see below chapter eight). Where children and young people receive information and explanations that do not fit their levels of cognitive development the scope for confusion is obvious. For some such confusion may be of minor significance, for others it can pose a barrier to the attainment of a realistic self-concept, and when accurate information is finally acquired, it may call for a search for self at the most fundamental level:

I knew my father was an American, and now my mother wasn't a New Zealander ... . Then I looked at the names she'd given me - my name. I don't know why, but it tugged at me in some way that I can't explain. It was this little person from way back then ...

(Rockel and Ryburn, 1988, p. 64)

Another study of interest in terms of the possible effects on identity formation of age-inappropriate explanations is that of McRoy and her colleagues (1988). This showed a major discrepancy sometimes between the views of adopted adolescents about when they were told that they had been adopted and those of their adopting parents, who maintained that their children had grown up with the knowledge that they were adopted.

This mismatch, as they indicate, can be explained most easily, not in terms of the truthfulness or otherwise of the respective parties, but rather as the consequence of explanations that did not fit the age of the child. The adolescents in question may well have been told when they were young of the fact that they were adopted. In the absence, however, of an explanation at the appropriate level of understanding, reinterpreted over time to take account of growing awareness, the realisation of adoption could still come as a shock, as it often did in middle childhood, when it resulted from something that someone else said. These situations could also create the need for a major reassessment of relationships and identity.

There are probably few adopting parents who do not these days talk to their children at some level about adoption, although the

Adoption White Paper, (199, p. 7-8, paras. 4.18, 4.25) proposes arrangements that would be likely to require of adopters that they undertake this task in a detailed and comprehensive way. This is a recognition of the fact that the degree of understanding necessary for full and proper comprehension is such that explanations offered on a "once for all basis" may not be very much help. There is also a fine balance between conveying information in the absence of any request, because absence of request may not mean lack of interest (Sachdev, 1991) and providing the right information when it is asked for, which may not be easy:

Of course you always imagine yourself talking to your child about this in the cosiest of possible circumstances. You're sitting by the fire in the evening and you've had a lovely read and you've talked and cuddled and then they say, "Mummy ... " and you give them all the right answers at the right time. Whereas in fact Martin was driving a carload of children to the cinema, and it was pouring wet, a cold winter's day and the car was all steamed up, and all of a sudden Lucy bawled out, "Why did my real mother not want me Daddy?". He was trying to make a difficult turn at the time, and he said he came out in a sweat.

(Rockel and Ryburn, 1988, p. 43)

The work of Brodzinsky and his colleagues (1984a, 1984b) also throws into some doubt the current practice of "doing" life [story] work with children without incorporating planning for the constant revision and updating of that work. The revision that we are talking about here is not so much the updating of events, something which may sometimes be regularly incorporated in life work; rather it is revision to accommodate changing levels of interest and understanding, and increasingly to create a continuity in the story between the "two lives" of pre- and post-adoption.

The potential that continuing contact can offer in seeing that the adoption story is a real one, which matches the cognitive level of children, scarcely needs to be stated.

Body image, awareness and identity

A key aspect of identity formation which has been identified by many, including Erikson (1959, p. 127), is the sense of "being at home in one's body". Developing a sense of physical awareness and difference is something that many theorists believe is a task that begins with the child's earliest social interaction (see for example Klein, 1932) and few would dispute that an acceptance of one's body (whatever its perceived limitations) is crucial in the process of identity formation. Once more, adolescence is a crucial time in the development of body image, and most adults can probably recall moments of agonising comparison at this stage of their lives. This comparison process begins much earlier, however, in the meanings that others give to each child's physical development, often with reference to other family members.

For some adopted people a lack of comparative information in relation to their original families may leave what feels like a significant gap. This may, as Triseliotis has observed (1991), complicate identity achievement. Although a number of adoption theorists and researchers, including Triseliotis (see for example Feigelman and Silverman, 1983; Frisk, 1964; Kowal and Schilling, 1985), have highlighted physical differences as a significant factor it has nonetheless received very little detailed attention from any of them.

Brodzinsky and his colleagues (1984a, 1984b) speculate, again drawing on Piaget (1963, 1964), that it is at the concrete operations stage that children not only differentiate between biological and adoptive parenting, but that they come to acquire an understanding and belief that biological connectedness between parent and child is the essence of what makes family. Adoptive status therefore creates, they claim, stress and a sense of confusion for children. This is naturally a time too, therefore, when physical comparisons begin to assume greater significance.

Lois Raynor's (1980) important retrospective longitudinal study of adopted people and their parents highlighted the fact that, both for parents and adoptees, adoption identity could be an unhappy one if there was a lack of likeness, and this sense of difference could contribute to a feeling of not belonging. A feeling of physical difference in their families of origin is not an uncommon one for adoptees. Even those who did not discover their adoptions until adulthood often report a particularly strong sense of difference (Rockel and Ryburn, 1988; Sorosky and Pannor, 1978).

For adopting parents without contact, the lack of comparative information about the "normal" physical development of their child in terms of their genetic inheritance may also place them at a disadvantage which potentially can contribute to lack of parenting confidence. Birth parents who subsequently have other children whom they themselves parent also miss the comparative information about their first child where there is no continuing contact. Lacking the yardsticks that can make second time parenting an easier task, and one more confidently entered taken on, they are instead placed at the disadvantage of being left with only the anxiety of unanswered questions.

For some adoptees nothing may be more pressing than questions about physical characteristics.

My questions were - Who did I look like? Where did my red hair come from? Why have I got freckles ...

(Rockel and Ryburn, 1988, p. 49)

We encountered in our study situations where the absence of physical likeness between adoptees and their adoptive families seemed sometimes to have created appreciable difficulty for adoptees in feeling they fully belonged. This is well summed up in the following excerpt from a video recorded interview:

Well, you felt inferior in lots of ways. You'd go into people's places after school and there'd be parents who just looked like their children, and in a way that sort of makes you feel not quite real, or as though you were sort of second best.

(Morrall and Ryburn 1986)

43

In the interview with Lynne and Andrea (see below chapter nine) Andrea describes how, even though she has had continuing contact with her birth daughter Annabel, now thirteen, for all her life, there had come a time recently when Annabel had wanted to compare their bodies, to look at hands, knees, feet and so on to establish her genetic inheritance. Detailed information of this sort, which may assume great importance in adolescence, is obviously only possible with contact.

Another aspect of body image and awareness that is seldom mentioned in the literature is the profound impact that meeting birth parents in adulthood can have on the self-concept of adoptees.

There are so many differences between adopted people and their adoptive families that you get used to difference. If you haven't had any contact with your birth family, then to suddenly be confronted by people who are like you - it just blew my mind. It also blew my birth family's mind. They also found it difficult to believe that there was this person who looked just so much like the rest of them.

(Rockel and Ryburn, 1988, p. 76)

The changes to self-concept that such meetings often bring also contribute to changes in the feelings adoptees may have about themselves, and in their self-esteem, as the following two extracts from interviews indicate:

... to see my next sister down looking so much like my daughter when she was a baby. It gave me a very warm feeling.

What really thrilled me about Sally [her birth mother] was that I could see her in me. And what it showed me is that you're more what you're born - you really are. I'd really felt like a fish out of water, that I didn't belong. I didn't recognise it at the time, but I can now.

(Rockel and Ryburn, 1988, p. 76)

44

Birth parents often similarly describe the profound effect of such meetings on their physical self-image.

We spent the weekend sort of sitting opposite one another and we noticed things - that we sat in the same way and our body language was similar and I kept having to go to look in the mirror again to see what I looked like because I couldn't remember ... we couldn't seem to remember what we looked like or how we fitted in, and we matched hands and feet and "who writes like this?" and all sorts of physical things. And I was quite surprised that the physical things were so strong, I always thought that they would be changed ...

(Morrall and Ryburn, 1986)

Though, as has been noted above, it has long been recognised that absence of similarity in physical characteristics could in some instances pose issues in terms of adoptive identity not only for children but also for their adopting parents, traditional adoption practice sought not to manage difference, but to obliterate it wherever possible. The concept of "matching" was often little more than a crude attempt to eliminate physical differences. The absurdity of this approach was highlighted by Sants (1964) and the "double-bind" that it created for adoptees was identified by Stone (1969). The acceptance of difference, as Kirk has emphasised (1964, 1981), rather than attempts to submerge it, does seem to be an important part of successful identity as an adoptive parent.

The reminders for adoptive parents that the children they parent do not share the same birth inheritance are, as I have written elsewhere (1991), a normal feature of their everyday life. Reminders may occur when other people who do not know of their children's adoption make physical comparisons with the adoptive parents, they may occur at the time of the arrival of a birth child in the wider family network, or as questions are being asked at the doctor's about a child's familial health history. This twenty-two year-old adoptee had one particular memory from when she was nine of how a sense of difference was brought home painfully to both her and her mother:

I remember being really hurt by the midwife when she said to my mother "you know what to do" - she was breast feeding and of course she'd never done that before and the midwife was really stroppy and said something to Mum like "Oh you must know what to do, you've fed other children". And I remember Mum saying, "she's actually my first, the other two are adopted". And I remember feeling really hurt and angry at that comment because I didn't want the midwife to know."

(previously unpublished interview extract, Rockel and Ryburn, 1988)

Reminders of difference may also come when a child demonstrates a skill, ability or characteristic that seems very far removed from those of the adopting parents. Paradoxically these reminders may also occur where children do mirror some of the qualities of their adoptive parents.

People were surprised to learn that our children were adopted because they looked so like us and were such nice kids. So there is a hidden and often unspoken expectation that adopted kids are different. I suppose it's the "bad blood" thing. I always found that very hurtful, and I used to get angry about it, and I guess protective. I felt helpless, because of course there's nothing you can do.

(Rockel and Ryburn, 1988, p. 40)

Physical differences in particular become obvious not only to adoptees but to their adoptive parents through opportunities for continuing contact in various forms, and for some this can contribute to a clearer sense of identity:

I came to see that really we were basing something on a pretence which we didn't need. It wasn't necessary to pretend that this was like any other family. This was our family, and it happened to be set up by adoption, and to me that was valid, and my feelings were just as strong as other parents'. Maybe different, but just as strong.

(Rockel and Ryburn, 1988, p. 44)

Other differences and identity achievement

In the main, where the issue of adoptees' perceptions of difference compared with their adoptive families has been noted, it has been exclusively in relation to physical characteristics, (see for example Feigelman and Silverman, 1983; Jaffe and Fanshel, 1970). We found in our study (Rockel and Ryburn, 1988) a wider range of differences identified by adoptees than have been reported elsewhere and an emphasis on purely physical differences seems a simplification. We were able also to learn from adoptees who had been reunited with birth relatives what identifications were important for them following reunion, and in this way perhaps gained additional insight into perceptions of difference before reunion. We discovered that for some adoptees a sense of difference did not centre on physical difference at all, rather it centred on a range of behavioural and personality characteristics, as the following interview excerpts illustrate.

I can actually remember at high school and particularly when I started to take an interest in things that were quite foreign to my parents because I have very few interests in common with them that I started to wonder then. I was at high school, and still am very interested in mechanical things, engineering type things and both my parents are completely awash there - there's nothing at all. ... I think I was also aware as I grew up of quite different personalities. I just didn't have any empathy for lots of their feelings. Their political thoughts, their intellectual sort of thinking, their career, their family attitudes, all sorts of things I found it just wasn't me and I was quite different. And I did wonder I think like most adoptees probably do, as I went through the teenage rebellion bit, is this normal or is it because I'm adopted and I remember that thought recurring a lot.

(previously unpublished interview extract, Rockel and Ryburn, 1988)

The differences between me and my family became more apparent as the years went by. We operated in quite different ways. I think that I am quite a feeling person, and I know my father especially doesn't operate at that level and my sister and I are completely different in terms of abilities, talents and things that we did, and we had a fairly stormy relationship most of the time.

(Rockel and Ryburn, 1988, p. 47)

I always felt very different. I remember as a child trying so hard to identify with them. Like I remember - I must have been four or five - really trying to identify with my father and going to rugby matches with him. I've always loathed and detested rugby - even as a kid I couldn't stand it. But I used to force myself to go with him. I hated it - it was boring, cold, long. Yet I used to go, because it was just a way of trying to belong.

(Rockel and Ryburn, 1988, p. 51)

These three extracts highlight how complex and subtle the search for identification in their adoptive families can be for some adoptees, and where the sought for correspondence either cannot be perceived, as in the case of the first two extracts, or achieved, as in the last, then a satisfying self-concept and sense of identity may be missing as well.

For some this sense of difference in relation to traits and characteristics can be brought home more as a consequence of experiences in adulthood, as both the adopted person below and the interview with Chris (see below chapter six) indicate, so that re-evaluations of adoptive identity in adult life may not be unusual.

I think the strongest feelings started to come out when I had my own children and started to watch them grow up. There would be things that I saw them doing that were obviously inherited from me, and I found that intriguing. For the first time in my life I could see a direct inherited link with a person, and I'd never seen that before. It suddenly dawned on me why people got enthusiastic about seeing inherited traits in children, and it was a whole new awakening - a whole piece of human experience that I'd never had before.

(Rockel and Ryburn, p. 48)

Adoption and loss

The perception of differences in terms of physical resemblance and personality characteristics and traits is only one part of a complex and interlocking process. The second part of that process is one of mourning. This is a diffuse grief process. The factor that most significantly compounds the sense of loss that may occur in adoption is the "living" nature of the bereavement. The act of separation from a still living original family does not have the finality of death. It has nothing of the tangibility of bereavement by death and nor does it have any of the rituals which all societies develop to aid the process of mourning (see for example Gorer, 1965; Hinton, 1967 ; Marris, 1974; Parkes, 1972).

In the absence of any continuing contact with the birth family however, the loss that adoption brings is just as final. As a loss that may be largely unacknowledged it may become more subtly pervasive than that occasioned by death, and more difficult therefore to grieve. There are two aspects to this bereavement.

The first is the physical loss of an original family. In so far as this parallels a bereavement by death its importance should be attended to properly, but perhaps but is unlikely to be. We could, for example, extrapolate from Brown and Harris's important research on the aetiology of depression in women (1978) that adoption, in paralleling the death of a parent in a child's early years, could constitute one important factor that might predispose women adoptees to the symptoms of depressive illness in adulthood.

I remember in my first marriage having an amazing argument with my husband one night. He seemed to be so secure in the knowledge of who he was and I actually remember saying to him, "It's OK for you, you know who you are, I don't know who I am. I still have that awful feeling. It's still there."

(previously unpublished interview, Rockel and Ryburn, 1988)

Men were not included in the Brown and Harris study, but they may be similarly affected. The diffuse but persistent feeling of abandonment that some adoptees, including those adopted in infancy, can experience in relation to the loss of birth relatives was poignantly expressed in interview by this forty-year-old man:

I have a feeling about myself that I've been quite sad all my life, with little pockets of forgetfulness and happiness. I seem to have gone along quite sadly, always looking for one person to be close to. I'm wondering now if that's got to do with a fact that I've just learned - that my birth mother looked after me for five months and breast-fed me for six weeks. When I was taken from my birth mother so that my adoptive Mum could practice looking after me, I cried and didn't stop until I got back into her arms.

(Rockel and Ryburn, 1988, p. 50)

An eighteen-year-old adoptee who had only recently met his ten-year-old half-brother indicated how the loss of a family through adoption is not only perceived as abandonment or rejection by adoptees themselves:

Him and I went for a walk on Thursday and he asked me questions, you know, "Why did Mum give you away?", "Didn't you like Mummy or didn't she like you when you were born?", and I didn't know how to answer them at all. So we went past a corner shop and I bought him a lollipop and that shut him up for a while. No, that sounds terrible but I just didn't know what to do, I was lost, even when he said to me "Why do you have to go into the army and get killed, there's all these wars but I've only just got to know you." And I felt like sort of hugging him and saying - "Oh isn't that sweet", but I'm reserved about a lot of things.

(previously unpublished interview, Rockel and Ryburn, 1988)

Seligman's research (1975), which led to his theory of "learned helplessness", would suggest that an experience of loss over which it was impossible to feel any sense of control leads to a reduced capacity to manage comparable situations in the future. There is an accompanying blow to any concept of self as someone who manages life and its decisions effectively and a resultant loss of self-esteem. The loss of an original family is one over which very few adoptees are in a position to exert any control, and loss of control over important life decisions can continue to be the life experience of some adoptees, as Chris identifies in the interview in chapter six, (see also Bertocci and Schechter, 1991).

The second aspect of loss of original family centres on what Sants, in 1964, termed "genealogical bewilderment". Sants used this term to describe the predicament and result for adoptees of growing up in substitute care without access to information about ancestry. Just as the absence of information about physical development may heighten perceptions of difference and complicate for some the task of achieving a complete sense of body image in their formation of identity, so can the absence of many other pieces of genealogical information. Kornitzer, writing in 1971, on the basis of her research, concluded that:

Background knowledge of one's family is like baby food - it is literally fed to a person as part of the normal nourishment that builds up his mental and emotional structure and helps the person become acquainted with what he is so that he can seize his inheritance of himself.

(p. 43)

Such information, as the interview excerpt below highlights, assumes particular meaning according to the social context. In this case, for example, it is the meaning that knowledge about other relatives has in the peer group that gives it its particular significance.

Where did my grandparents come from? All my friends had uncles or grandparents who came from really interesting places, and I always wanted something like that to hang on to.

(Rockel and Ryburn, 1988, p. 49)

For others "bewilderment" centres on the lack of a way to understand themselves in terms of attributes and skills.

No, I've never had any great feelings to want to look like anybody really. No there's not that ... I suppose I'm looking for natural attributes that I may have and I suppose as you grow up ... as you make decisions about a job and career and everything and you look for strengths and things you might have or expertise in certain areas and you wonder what inherited strengths you have, and of course knowing that is part of knowing your ancestry.

(previously unpublished interview, Rockel and Ryburn, 1988)

I sometimes have this feeling that I'm missing something, and I haven't found it. Maybe it's music - it could be anything. I think I've searched, in a limited way, to find that thing, but never have, and possibly never will.

(Rockel and Ryburn, 1988, p. 52)

Others describe their lack of any sense of self which is grounded in a family of origin in much more global ways. It is for them something which potentially mediates many other aspects of identity.

It was like floating around in a swimming pool with nothing to grab hold of so I could stop still and say, "Well here is where I am and here is where I've come from." I didn't have that reference point.

(Rockel and Ryburn, 1988, p. 53)

It was like you had nothing to anchor on to. You had nothing you could grasp onto and say, well that's definitely me because I can see that in my parents so I know that's part of me.

(previously unpublished interview, Rockel and Ryburn, 1988)

In his paper Sants (1964) uses the Andersen fairy story of the ugly duckling as a metaphor for the identity confusion that for some may be resolved only through physical meeting. In our study (Rockel and Ryburn, 1988) we met many adoptees and birth parents for whom only the opportunity to meet brought resolution to their "bewilderment". As Chris remarks in her interview (see below chapter six) other forms of information, such as photographs, may never offer for some what they really want - they are merely an essentially unsatisfying "glimpse of a life".

Images of original families

Where there has been bereavement by death, grief resolution, if it is achieved, would seem to come about as the consequence of internalising an image of the dead person that is satisfying and complete (Kubler-Ross, 1975; Parkes, 1972). For adoptees, similarly, the achievement of a positive sense of identity may depend on the internalisation of a satisfying and accurate image of original family members. The extent to which this can happen is likely to centre on how realistic the images are that they both receive and come to believe concerning their original families. Lack of information and contact do not seem to fit the rule of the old adage "out of sight out of mind" (see for example Lifton, 1979). Adoptees enter into a life-time relationship with their birth families, whether or not there is contact.

I think the thing that would really upset me would be if she turned out to be nothing like me, because all these years that's how I've connected her to me.

(previously unpublished interview, Rockel and Ryburn, 1988)

In the absence of continuing information there is clearly more scope for images of original families which are divorced from reality, and in some instances this may create intrusive preoccupations that might interfere in identity formation.

I used to think that she might wear leather jackets and be riding around on the back of a bike with this guy with a long beard. And when I found out that she was tall like me, I used to look at every tall woman ... the right age, and think "I wonder if that's her".

(Rockel and Ryburn, 1988, p. 49)

Birth parents often describe similar concerns (see for example Howe *et al*, 1992) so that they are:

...forever looking under pram hoods to see if it was her, or looking on the swings at the park.

(Rockel and Ryburn, 1988, p. 165)

Neither are adoptive parents immune from such preoccupations:

*... but then we couldn't not know, we couldn't not **feel** that they had come from somewhere. And you can't divorce yourself from the person that brought your child into the world, no matter how hard you try.*

(Rockel and Ryburn, 1988, p. 49)

Even where the past has been difficult or is painful to come to terms with, as one adopted person quoted by Triseliotis (1992, p. 39) put it, "Trust is always better than deception. No one should have the right to erase part of another person's self ... ".

There is a wealth of research which indicates that the environment, attitudes and values of the home can be of key importance in shaping and influencing identity formation (see for example Feldman and Eliott [eds.], 1990). In adopting families the attitudes, values and beliefs espoused by parents will encompass also a view of children's original families. The attitudes of adopters to birth families have been shown to be important in several studies. In an Australian study Rickarby and Egan (1980) found that adoptive parents who experienced difficulties in their relationships with their children tended to explain these in terms of their children's adverse birth heritage and "to question the rightness of the decision to adopt" (p. 472). Kaye and Warren (1988) identified a similar tendency in their study of the processes of communication in adoptive families. They showed that the more frequently families experienced problems, the more likely they were to attribute them to adoption. This was confirmed in the study I undertook with Jenny Rockel (1988).

When I went and got pregnant myself my parents were really horrible and unsupportive about it. I think in a way being adopted made me really really alienated from them at times like that. If your parents blame you and don't help you when things go wrong it's horrible, but when they're not even your real parents it brings home to you all these other realisations they've been telling you, you know, about how you came into the world and why you were adopted.

(previously unpublished interview extract Rockel and Ryburn, 1988)

There are at least three studies which indicate that where adopters acquire and pass on negative messages to their children concerning their original families, these messages may pose significant difficulties for adoptees in the achievement of positive identity in adolescence. McWhinnie, on the basis of her research, concludes that such negative messages may lead to delinquency and anti-social behaviour (1969). Frisk's study (1964) described the effects of negative messages in terms of reduced self-esteem, and Raynor (1980) reported similar negative consequences in her follow-up study. We also confirmed that for some adoptees the application of negative messages to their original families carried a labelling effect for them as well:

I couldn't talk with my mother, not even about my period or anything like that. When I did get it it was really horrible. It was like "now she's ready to go out and be like her mother". When I was a child I used to try to tell myself that I wasn't bad, and I wasn't the person she said I was going to be. But I found myself turning that way when I left home, and all the things that my mother said I was going to do as far as men were concerned, I've done them. All my friends lost respect for me and after a while I found myself not caring what anyone else thought. But I did care, really.

(Rockel and Ryburn, 1988, p. 52)

I have written elsewhere (1991), of the difficulty that can exist for adopting parents, where there has been no first hand meeting, in acquiring positive images of the original families of their children when those children have joined them as the result of contested proceedings, or difficult or traumatic events in their first families. In situations where there have been contested court proceedings, information will have been filtered in order to maximise the chance of "winning" a case. This process is likely to distort the images for all who are involved. Social workers, who by no means always initially have poor relationships with original families, can seldom salvage much of this relationship at the end of what is almost inevitably a bitter court battle (Ryburn, 1992b). Yet these are the same workers who will be the principal source of information for adopting families, in the absence of contact, concerning the children who are placed with them. It would be asking a lot in such circumstances for new families to acquire other than negative views about original families (Ryburn, 1992a). Where adopting parents have negative images of original families it is probably impossible for them not to convey these to their children, whether by word or silence. For children in such circumstances it is but a short step, with growing awareness of heredity, to internalise these as messages that can apply also to themselves.

Continuing contact offers a way to overcome situations in which children are likely to gain only negative messages about their original families. No family is without positive attributes, though these may easily be buried in the court process. Fratter's work (1989) and my own recent study (1994, in preparation), have shown that even where children have been adopted following very difficult circumstances, such contact can work to enrich the lives of all.

Discrimination, stigma and identity
Adopted people
When those who are not adopted perceive differences in themselves this may not be as problematic as it was for the adoptees above. Indeed the enhancement of self-esteem may follow from positive feelings about individual uniqueness. It is not only in the inner world that perception of difference can create problems in positive identity formation, however, for negatively connoted differences in the social world are the

foundation of discrimination. Goffman's work (1963) constitutes an important theoretical study of the effects of social discrimination [stigma] on personal identity. He maintains that:

The more a stigmatised individual deviates from the norm, the more wonderfully he may have to express possession of the standard subjective self if he is to convince others that he possesses it, and the more they may demand that he provide them with a model of what an ordinary person is supposed to feel about himself.

(p. 41)

Goffman's assertion is supported in the research which seems to demonstrate that the achievement of a clear sense of personal identity is a struggle against the odds for those that are victims of discrimination, (see for example Stiffman and Davis [eds.], 1990, for discussion of some of the issues for young people from ethnic minorities; for identity issues in relation to discrimination for those persons with disabilities, see Morris, 1991; see McEwan [ed.], 1990 in relation to discrimination and identity achievement in elders).

Adopted people suffer both subtle and overt discrimination at times. This may be in terms of the legislation. As was noted, for example, in chapter one, even after reform in the 1949 and 1958 Adoption Acts, inheritance rights are still not entirely equal, access to identifying information about original families is available in some instances only after counselling, and this information is denied to children and young people. Alternatively, discrimination may be in relation to social attitudes, which value blood kinship over social kinship.

Social discrimination for adoptees exists in both childhood and adulthood:

One day one of my friends said, "Oh, I heard the funniest thing the other day - they told me you were adopted!" And she laughed and laughed, and I said, "What's so funny. It's true." I don't know why, but somehow people used to find it really incredible

- people who didn't know much about it. They thought it was really weird and mysterious."

I was just aware that other people made the distinction. There were "children", and there were "adopted children", and there was a difference. Adopted children weren't quite "proper" children. Once when I called in to see Dad at work, I heard someone say, "That's Frank's son, did you know? Well he's not really, he's adopted".

As a child, I had a vague sense of not being included in things, but it really came out in the open after my parents died. An aunt came to me and my sister and asked for a brooch that had been in my father's family. "I think it should be kept in the Thompson family", she said. My sister and I were most indignant because we felt we were Thompsons. But it was very obvious that we weren't regarded as family.

(Rockel and Ryburn, 1988, pp. 48 - 49)

There are key stages in the life cycle (in Western society at least) when we seem particularly vulnerable to distinctions which create difference. Adolescence is a period when the process of individuation means that peer group identity is particularly important, though this is not to imply that the peer group and its values are necessarily at odds with mainstream adult values (Coleman, 1974; Coleman and Hendry, 1990). The process of peer conformity is actually aided by that of stigmatisation. As Goffman (1963, p. 41) notes, stigmatisation creates the need for extra effort to conform to the model of normality. Thus the struggles to belong of those who are singled out as different provide a focus for the majority that diverts group attention away from any questions concerning their own conformity to the norm. There is also in addition, of course, an investment by the majority in maintaining the status of difference of those who have been singled out.

The struggle for the status of 'normality' can sometimes create a major disjunction between how a person who feels stigmatised believes they will be viewed by others, and the reality. Elements of their identity which may once, in childhood for example, have set them apart from their peers, may have lost any great significance for the adult peer group, but the sense of difference and not belonging may remain. Where aspects of identity are formed around such misconceptions they can sometimes create significant fears and difficulties in managing social relationships.

Just before we were married I thought I'd better mention it [adoption] to her family and they sort of shrugged it off, and I was quite surprised that they thought it was nothing, whereas I thought it could have been quite a major stumbling block whether I got to the altar or not.

(Morrall and Ryburn, 1986)

This thirty-four-year-old man recorded in interview the effect that the label of social difference had had on him. He experienced it as a cumulative effect that continued to get worse to the point where:

I felt I couldn't get friendly with people for long, or trust people, 'cause they'd let you down.

(Morrall and Ryburn, 1986)

For this man it was only the opportunity to meet his mother in adulthood that took away the feeling of difference that had become so acute over the years. When he first met his mother he described the feeling as a sense of identity achievement:

... I suddenly felt "normal", you know sort of as though everything had come together. ... sort of "good" as though you were just part of the human race ...

(Morrall and Ryburn, 1986)

Birth parents
Birth parents probably face the greatest overt discrimination, with its resultant effects on self-esteem and the ability to

acquire a positive self-image. Those who relinquish children find that their experience is often not talked about in an open way so that they may be left with an overwhelming sense of unreality about their lives.

Nobody who knew me came up to me and said "How was the birth?". The whole thing and the pregnancy was completely ignored .... Nobody wanted to talk about it with me .... I didn't realise that other people possibly in the same circumstances were suffering in the same way that I was too .... I thought there must be something fundamentally wrong with me, and I just suffered alone.

(Morrall and Ryburn, 1986)

When I did my nursing training later I realised that the way that I had had my baby was the way people used to deliver stillbirths. It was quiet, hushed, nobody dared talk, and the mother never saw the baby. I suppose it was a stillbirth really because it wasn't my baby - I wasn't going to have it - and everybody was embarrassed and didn't know what to say.

(Rockel and Ryburn, 1988, p. 27)

Those who lose their children through contested adoptions face probably the greatest social discrimination. We live in a society which ascribes enormous value to being a parent and to discharging the tasks of parenting effectively. The intervention of the State to transfer that task permanently to other parents in contested adoption is a very public statement of failure that brings with it guilt, remorse and the condemnation of others (Howe *et al*, 1992; Ryburn, 1992b; Ryburn, 1994, in preparation). It can lead to an enormous assault on identity:

The stigmatising that I feel as a result of all this, I have felt almost not a man any more. I haven't had a relationship since that time because I thought to myself what have I got to offer any more.

(Ryburn, 1992b, p. 37)

We had to move from where we were living on the Brockwell. It wasn't things people said, it was the way they used to look at me that was worse, at the shops or the laundry or even just in the street. Without Dave I couldn't stand it any more.

(Ryburn, in preparation)

Though nothing can diminish the tragedy, from all perspectives, of situations when children and their original families are compulsorily separated, the single thing that birth parents identify in these circumstances as most likely to help in the reintegration of their lives and the establishment of a clearer sense of identity is the possibility for some continuing exchange of first-hand information, (Ryburn, in preparation).

Any information, anything at all would help. How can I go on like they're dead when I know they're alive.

(Ryburn, in preparation)

Adoptive parents

Adoptive parents can also suffer discrimination. This is often but not always more subtle. It ranges sometimes from differential treatment over maternity and paternity leave, especially where an older child joins the family, to sensing exclusion as not a "real" parent at sessions or events for parents and children. It is not unusual for adopting parents to recount how the task of incorporating the role of parent in identity formation seems more difficult as a consequence of believing that having been assessed as "good enough" to parent their children they must discharge their parenting responsibilities in exemplary fashion.

When I knew that my marriage was going to have to finish, it made it much more painful. I was always so aware of my responsibility to all the children, but somehow having adopted children is an added responsibility. You've willingly and knowingly taken on the care and love of somebody else's children, and that's something I found incredibly hard to come to terms with. I think I've had more of a sense of failure perhaps because of the tremendous standards I set myself as the parent of adopted children.

(Rockel and Ryburn, 1988, p. 155)

Adopting parents who have continuing contact with their children's original families can report (see below, chapter four) a diminution of that added sense of responsibility, since they feel a confidence that derives from being approved in their parenting role by their children's original family. Their self-concept as adopters becomes clearer, and they feel better about their role in parenting a child who was born to others.

Ethnicity and identity

For adopted children who are of mixed ethnic parentage and from minority ethnic communities and their families, there are particular difficulties surrounding identity. Unlike an (usually) assigned component of identity such as adoption, ethnicity is most often a highly visible characteristic. The achievement of positive ethnic identity, where there is adoption, has, because of this visibility, perhaps even greater urgency than the incorporation of positive beliefs and feelings about being adopted, though clearly the two exist in a dynamic relationship.

In any society where the norms, values, and social institutions are not fairly representative of all sections of the community there will be discrimination. Where ethnic minorities are excluded from equal participation there is racism. Racism helps to create unequal life chances for children in social environments, including health, education and vocational opportunity. There is overwhelming evidence from a wide variety of sources that those from ethnic minorities in the United Kingdom are systematically disadvantaged in health (see for example Torkington, 1991), housing (see for example *Social Trends*, 1992), employment and the labour market (see for example DSS, 1992; Bhatt [ed.] 1988), income maintenance (see for example NACAB, 1991) and in the application of the law where there has been discrimination (see for example CRE, 1992). Where racism exists the establishment of ethnic identity and pride is an additional burden placed on children of minority groups. Phinney and her colleagues (1990) suggest that an ability to manage and deal with racism is the major prerequisite for the establishment of a satisfying ethnic identity within overall identity formation.

There is a substantial body of research that indicates the crucial role of family in creating the foundation for ethnic pride and the formation of a personal identity which includes positive ethnic identity (see for example Harrison, 1985; Jaynes and Williams, 1989; Peters, 1985; Spencer, 1983; Spencer and Dornbusch, 1990). Whether, when children from minority ethnic groups are adopted, they find in their new families an environment that creates the preconditions for a sense of ethnic pride and self-worth may therefore be critical in determining their achievement of a broader sense of positive self-identity.

The research indicates (Aboud 1987; Davey, 1983; Hogg *et al*, 1987; Ogbu, 1987) that in general it is hard for those who belong to ethnic minority groups to develop a clear and positive sense of their ethnic identity, and often there may be a wish for identification with the dominant culture. Such identification is clearly not consistent with strong ethnic identity, and within the context of the norms for the ethnic group to which they belong it is behaviour that can reasonably be described as "abnormal".

Transracial placements
The research of Barn (1990) and of Rowe and her colleagues (1989) indicates differences in treatment of black families in terms of the relatively higher proportion of African Caribbean children who enter short-term State care. Barn has found (1993) higher numbers overall of black children in the care system. Rowe and her colleagues did not find this to be the case where long term care was considered (1989). There are findings that indicate alarmingly higher rates of adoption for black children of mixed ethnic parentage (Charles *et al*, 1992; Rowe *et al*, 1989; Thoburn *et al*, 1992). The study, still in progress, of Thoburn and her colleagues of 246 black children and black children of mixed ethnic parentage (plus for some research purposes another 37 added later to the sample) indicates that these children as a total group are more likely to

be separated in adoption from their siblings, and that their placements are more likely to disrupt. Eighty-seven per cent of the sample of black children of mixed ethnic parentage (159) were transracially placed with white parents; in the total sample only twenty-two per cent of placements were same race placements.

Unfortunately there are no national statistics that can tell us whether this figure, deriving from a study of an overall sample of 1,165 adoption and permanent care placements made by 24 voluntary agencies in England, Scotland and Wales between 1980 and the end of 1984, might reasonably be extrapolated to give an overall picture of the percentage of adopted black children who are transracially placed. However, the geographical spread of the agencies and the fact that voluntary agencies have often been at the forefront of same race placement policies might reasonably lead to the conclusion that this is not an over-estimate for this period. It is difficult to say to what extent growing recognition of the importance for children of their ethnic and cultural heritage may have altered this picture since 1984, and Barn in her study (pp. 63-4) notes that in Wenford, where her study was conducted, there are now few transracial placements, but she expresses concern for the many children placed transracially before there was a same race placement policy.

The historical context

Transracial placements, which almost invariably entail the placement of black children and black children of mixed ethnic parentage in white families, have been a source of concern for more than two decades. The one-way nature of such placements (black children with white families) has, with some justification, led black opponents of transracial placements to regard them as a form of cultural genocide (see for example Chimuzie, 1975).

Ladner points out (1977) that it was many years after the beginning of legal adoption before black children began to be viewed as adoptable. When they were, as she points out, it corresponded with a decline, from the late 1960s, in the number of healthy white babies available for adoption. The British Adoption Project (BAP) from the mid 1960s sought to demonstrate that families could be found for the many black children in unplanned public care. Black families did not prove easy (for a largely white service) to recruit, and increasingly black children came to be regarded as difficult to place. At the same time the need for family was seen to be more important than the need for a family that was also black, and in the years from the late 1960s the practice of transcultural and transracial adoption became established. The Soul Kids campaign in the late 1970s and the New Black Families Project in the early 1980s, did demonstrate that black families could be found for black children deemed to be in need of adoption, and by the late 1970s there was the beginning of concerted opposition to transracial placement.

However, the disproportionately high numbers of black children in the care system (see for example Lambert, 1970; Lambert and Rowe, 1973), combined with the absence in most areas of effective strategies for recruiting black families, meant that transracial adoption carried on largely unabated. Even though many agencies now subscribe to practice policies concerning the same race placement of children and find moderate levels of support for doing so in both Department of Health Guidance (1990) and the Children Act 1989 (Section 22), many children who are black, including those of mixed ethnic parentage, have the option in adoption of only transracial placements.

Research about transracial placement
Opponents of transracial placement advance a number of important arguments at the heart of which is the issue of whether white parents of black children (including children of mixed ethnic parentage) can ever equip their children for life in a society "which is significantly racist in its attitudes and its distribution of opportunities" (Gill and Jackson, 1983, p. 136). The issue is wider than that of the goodwill and intentions of adopters, they would say. It is whether anyone who has not suffered racism, can create a sufficient sense of common purpose with children who inevitably will do so, in order to help them to cope with it. Only pride and a clear sense of ethnic

identity will be sufficient, it is argued, to enable satisfactory overall identity formation and survival in adulthood in a racist environment. These arguments are cogent and they find some support in the general research concerning ethnic identification as part of the overall achievement of a positive self-identity (see for example Phinney *et al*, 1989; Rotheram and Phinney, 1987).

The balance of research to date, however, on transracial adoption, which in some American studies (see for example Feigelman and Silverman, 1983) also includes what in the United Kingdom we call inter-country adoption, indicates that on general measures of self-esteem and personal adjustment transracial adoptees probably do as well as those who are not transracially adopted (see for example Gill and Jackson, 1983; McRoy *et al*, 1982; Simon and Alstein, 1977, 1981, 1987, 1992). There is some evidence, however, from a United Kingdom study of a clinical population (Howe and Hinings, 1987; cited in Thoburn, 1990) that families who have adopted transracially may be significantly over-represented amongst those seeking professional help because of behaviour problems in adopted children and young people. In half of their sample of 261 families who enquired about professional help, the family's race was known to the agency and in half of these instances there had been transracial placements.

It is reasonable to treat the general findings of positive adjustment in transracial adoption with a degree of caution. In the first place it is important to note that even in the most comprehensive longitudinal study (Simon and Alstein, 1992) the adoptees had only reached late adolescence. One of the persistent arguments of those opposed to transracial placements has always been that though adoptive families may mediate the effects of racism for their children during childhood, it is in adulthood that it will pose the greatest threat to self-concept, self-esteem and the achievement of a positive sense of personal identity (Chestang 1972; Chimuzie, 1975; Small 1986). One factor to note about transracial placements is that, like adoption in general, it is often a transfer of children across wealth barriers so that, for example, adopters in the Simon and Alstein study (p. 200) live in "middle- and upper-middle-class" neighbourhoods. These are neighbourhoods in which we can reasonably assume few of the original families of their adopted children would have lived. The comparative affluence of adopters may also be a factor that helps them to shield their children during childhood from the worst effects of racism and discrimination. The crisis that transracial placement might pose for some young black people who have been transracially placed, as they enter adulthood and confront a less sheltered world, is well summed up in the comments of an eighteen year old in a video recorded interview who stated that he now lacked confidence in who he was and that:

When the black community, the black person ... detects that depth of insecurity in me then I feel I want to stand back.

(Barnardos, 1988)

There is a critical need for studies which follow transracial adoptees into adulthood before we can say with any certainty that as a 'whole of life' experience transracial placement has not affected them adversely. The only longitudinal study which will provide any data on transracial adoptees in adulthood is that of Simon and Alstein (1993, in preparation) and even this will only provide information about adoptees in their early to middle twenties. McRoy and her colleagues (1982; 1983; 1984) compared 30 white families who had transracially adopted with 30 black children placed in black families. Using the self-esteem component of the Tennessee Self-Concept Scale they came to the conclusion that significant differences in self-esteem scores could not be found between the two groups. They also found, however, that transracially placed adoptees who had been raised in predominantly white areas had more negative stereotypes of the black community, though their self-esteem scores were not correspondingly low. They conclude (1983) that self-esteem and positive ethnic identification may operate as independent dimensions.

The question that remains unanswered is that which has been posed above. Will it be possible for self-esteem and ethnic-identification to operate independently of each other in adulthood, when the social disadvantages that confront minority communities impact more clearly and when family can operate as less of a 'buffer zone'? We must also question whether transracial adoptees who have negative views of the wider black community can reasonably be termed as essentially well adjusted by researchers (see for example Gill and Jackson, 1983).

There is a consistent finding across several research studies both in the United States and the United Kingdom which indicates, as McRoy and her colleagues (1983) found, that significant numbers of transracially placed adoptees may grow up without acquiring a strong and positive sense of ethnic identity. Gill and Jackson (1983) studied 53 British African Caribbean young people who had been placed transracially. They described them as, "made white in all but skin colour" (p. 137) and as having no contact with the black community. These young people's method of coping lay in "denying their racial background" and they seemed not to have "developed a sense of racial identity". Andujo (1988), studying the transracial adoptions of Mexican American adolescents placed in white families, found that they significantly lacked a clear sense of ethnic identity. Shireman and Johnson (1986) and Johnson and colleagues (1987) conducted a study of eight-year-olds which compared twenty-six black children in same race placements and a similar number who had been placed transracially. They reported a somewhat less developed sense of ethnic identity in those placed transracially compared with those placed in black families.

It is difficult to argue that lack of ethnic identity is desirable. To the extent that positive ethnic identity is, as Phinney and her colleagues have suggested (1990), a vital component in the ability to combat racism effectively, and ultimately vital in the overall formation of a strong sense of personal identity (a matter on which there is currently insufficient evidence to draw conclusions), there is a need for better placement planning, resourcing and recruiting. The research seems consistently to indicate that the attitudes of transracial adopters are significant in shaping their children's achievement of positive ethnic identity. In Grow and Shapiro's study of 125 African American children who had been transracially placed (1974) they found in interviews with adopters that the most positive attitudes on the part of parents to their children's ethnic communities related to the strongest sense of ethnic identity on the part of children. McRoy and her colleagues came to a similar conclusion (1982) and also highlighted the importance that living in multi-cultural communities could hold for the development of positive ethnic identity. It is significant to note that in Gill and Jackson's study (1983), where there was a marked lack of positive ethnic identification amongst adoptees, many adopters who had lived in multicultural communities had moved to predominantly white areas.

The primary justification for transracial placements has never centred strictly on their efficacy, though it does seem that some researchers, such as Bagley (1993), are moving almost to a position which he describes as "interculturalism" where transracial placements are recommended for their capacity to break down cultural barriers. Bagley portrays this concept as a new and positive development (p. 296), but in his description of it as a trend in race relations which leads to "rapid absorption" (p. 296) of immigrant groups, it seems indistinguishable in all but name from the widely discredited assimilationist policies of the 1960s.

It does seem that white adopters who are able positively to accept that their child has an entirely different ethnic inheritance and who live in multi-racial communities may well be able to help their children to develop positive attitudes to their own ethnic heritage. We should note however that Simon and Alstein's study (1992, pp. 200-201) indicates that attempts by adopters to develop ethnic pride in their children tend to wane over the years and in their study parents decided "that the one-culture family was an easier route" (p. 200). In addition, as Thoburn cautions (1990, p. 56), this finding comes largely from North American studies in a society which is culturally more pluralistic. United Kingdom research does not to date yield examples of adopters able to work effectively in helping transracially adopted children to achieve positive ethnic identification.

Justification for transracial placements has centred principally on the fact that not to make such placements will leave black children adrift in public care without permanent families. Delay in finding permanent families for children has long been acknowledged as harmful (see for example Rowe and Lambert, 1973). Feigelman and Silverman (1983) found in their study that delay in placement was a significant factor impeding the adjustment of transracial adoptees. To argue simply, however, that in the absence of sufficient same race placements transracial placements should be sought (Pinker, 1993) is to avoid crucial moral and political considerations.

Poverty and transracial placements
We know from a number of sources that poverty is the single factor most associated with admissions of children to all kinds of substitute care (see for example Bebbington and Miles, 1990) and as a determinant of those who will require social services (Becker and MacPherson, 1986; Becker and Silburn, 1990). It was estimated by Becker and McPherson (1986) in a large scale study that eighty-eight per cent of those receiving services from local authorities, which included therefore families whose children were in care, lived on or below the margins of poverty. The number of poor families as a percentage of the population has steadily increased since then (Bradshaw, 1990; *The Independent*, 19 July 1993) and it is reasonable to expect the percentage of poor families with children in care will also have increased. We know in addition that those from minority ethnic groups are over represented amongst those who live in poverty (see for example Amin and Oppenheim, 1992) and that black children of mixed ethnic parentage are especially vulnerable to admission to care (Bebbington and Miles, 1989). Together these factors create a major moral imperative to address the structural inequality that creates poverty and which gives rise to circumstances in which both white and black children are deemed to be in need of permanent new families by way of adoption.

A related moral issue is the amount of financial support that is available to poor families in parenting their children. Poor families, and black families who are poor amongst them, must view with bitter dismay the support and help that is given to foster families and adoptive families (by way of adoption allowances) to care for the children for whom they themselves may desperately have wanted to continue to care. Currently a family living on Income Support, receives an allowance of fifteen pounds and five pence for looking after a child of ten years. The National Foster Care Association in the United Kingdom recommends a minimum foster care allowance of sixty-three pounds for a ten-year-old. The State benefit for a fifteen-year-old is twenty-two pounds and fifteen pence, and the minimum recommended foster care allowance for a fifteen year old is seventy-four pounds. The National Foster Care Association figures include no element of reward or salary and are determined by the actual cost of bringing up a child. In fact since local authorities often pay enhanced rates to foster carers the actual per capita spending on foster care across all ages in England in 1990 - 1991 was one-hundred-and-two pounds per child per week, (Verity, 1993). This compares with an average child care allowance across all ages of approximately eighteen pounds received by those living on Income Support. Many families, including black families whose children are later adopted, could reasonably claim that with a commensurate level of financial support there would be no need for any form of permanent placement, whether or not this was transracial.

Legal adoption as an alien concept
A final consideration that is discussed in more detail in chapter four, should briefly be mentioned. Permanency planning philosophies, as the Short Report (p. 78) notes[1] have contributed to a perception of adoption as the most desirable form of permanent placement. This is not supported in the research, when measures such as comparative disruption rates for other forms of permanent placement are considered (Fratter *et al*, 1991). The emphasis on adoption as the preferred means

---

[1] See also *Review of Adoption Law*, 1992, p. 14, para. 6.1.

of permanency ignores the fact that the very concept of adoption as a complete and irrevocable legal transfer of a child from one family to another, especially where this has occurred against family consent, can be largely alien to black cultures. The Koran for example, whilst permitting the 'rescue' of abandoned children, forbids adoption (Benet, 1976, p. 27) and many Muslim countries have no provision in law for adoption. In other cultures, too, legal adoption has no place:

In the West Indies there would be no need to adopt a child to give them a sense of security - the child would know the relatives, the natural parents would know that the child was with that family. They would also have some input into that child's behaviour in that the "parent" could refer to the natural parent on any point of discipline. It would be very much a "loose" adoption. There is permanency but there would be no need for formal adoption.

Quite Honestly I never heard the word "adoption", before I came to England.

(Fratter, 1988, p. 68).

If the very fact of legal adoption does violence to cultural norms and traditions, then it can be argued that this will potentially render more difficult the achievement of ethnic identity within the framework of adoption. Where legal adoption is an alien concept this is also likely to be a major factor militating against the recruitment of adopters from minority ethnic communities. It therefore, in circular fashion, may be likely to lead to the continuance of transracial adoption on a large scale, unless alternative forms of placement are sought for black children who are seen to need new permanent families.

There are additional tasks in the achievement of a positive sense of identity for those from minority ethnic groups. The research evidence indicates that family influence is crucial in helping young people to achieve a positive sense of ethnic identity. A major task in the achievement of such an identity is the ability to manage and combat racism (Phinney *et al*, 1990). Where young people are placed transracially it seems that there can be difficulties in acquiring a positive ethnic identity. It may be that when we have the advantage of studies of transracial adoptees in adult years, research will show that while adoptees who did not develop a positive sense of ethnic identity were protected in their adoptive family environments from the effects of discrimination and social isolation, that in managing adult life with similar success there is significantly more difficulty.

Conclusion
It is the development of a clear sense of personal identity that permits us to enter future situations in our lives with a measure of confidence and assurance. It will be a key determinant of how we tackle new things, how successful we are in doing so, and how resilient we will be if things go wrong.

The achievement of a clear sense of personal identity is more difficult for those who have been adopted. Adoption creates interrelated but different issues for adopted people, birth parents and adoptive parents. It is clear from the evidence from many sources that for all parties secrecy and lack of information and a sense of discontinuity may add a further dimension of difficulty. The open exchange of information, most easily achieved through contact, so that it is readily available and not offered on a once and for all basis, is the single factor most likely to assist in the achievement of adoption identity and a positive sense of self-identity.

4 Research into contact and permanent placement

Introduction

This chapter focuses on the research in relating to open adoption and open practice in adoption. Traditionally Western adoption has comprised an economic motivation to transfer the care of children from the public to the private purse and a conviction that the state can best protect and promote the interests of those regarded as incapable of making their own decisions. The problem for the consumers of adoption has often been that, however well intentioned the decisions made about them may be, there has often been no, or at best minimal consultation with them.

In this context openness in adoption is perhaps most usefully seen, not in terms of policy and practice, but rather as a set of ideas and beliefs which stem from the attempts of some consumers and adoption professionals to re-channel the traditional flow of power in much 20th century Western adoption. For these people there is a central belief that the maintenance of some degree of contact in adoption, where there is consumer control over the process, will have for all parties significant advantages over a system which is led by professionals and based on the customary severance of all contact between birth families and adopting families. Openness in this context represents not only a model for practice but also an ideological commitment to challenge the belief that professionals "know best".

Social workers and other practitioners who wish to find a way to restore to adoption consumers full rights to participate in the decisions about their own lives can face two major obstacles. First, a practice culture which may fail fully to take account of the fact that adoption is both for present and for future time, so that decisions taken in the light of present knowledge and understanding require the flexibility to accommodate changing future circumstances. Second, the thinking that openness in adoption has only advantages to offer birth parents and that the gains for other parties to adoption will be minimal.

The contact between the parties to an adoption, where there is openness, may take many forms. It may range from the occasional exchange of letters and cards via an agency through to more direct contact by exchange of audio and video tapes, telephone calls or face to face meetings in which an intermediary is no longer necessary. Within this range of contact there will also of course be wide variation in the frequency and duration of contact, from annual contact by post through to the frequent informal contact that is described in chapter ten.

It is important to stress that contact, when there is openness, is evolutionary as any relationship is. The initial contact that the parties may agree on can be vastly different from the contact that may develop over time. Relationships in open adoption are thus renegotiated continuously, though the general trend is usually from formal or semi-formal contact to much more informal contact in which the facilitation of an agency is no longer necessary (see for example Iwanek, 1987; McRoy, 1988).

The contact between Annabel and her birth mother Andrea, with whom there are interviews in chapters eight and nine offers a good example. There were initial meetings between all of the parties at the time of placement, and there followed several years of contact by letter. The adoptive parents sent Andrea regular letters updating her on Annabel 's progress and also photographs of Annabel and her family. They would always send letters at milestones such as Annabel's birthday or at Christmas, but they sent many other letters which did not necessarily relate to any special event in Annabel's life. Andrea also sent regular letters to Annabel and her family informing them of changes and developments in her life. As Annabel grew up she would also draw pictures and make things for Andrea which would be posted to her. At this point in their relationship all of the letter contact was via the agency that arranged the original placement.

When Annabel was five years old Andrea decided that she felt confident and comfortable enough with the idea of meeting with Annabel and her family and asked the agency to make this request for her. Annabel's adoptive parents welcomed the contact. Initially Annabel and her mother met Andrea at a neutral setting in town and then subsequently the whole family met Andrea together with Andrea's boyfriend. Since that time there developed informal contact which the parties negotiated directly. There would be telephone contact which could be initiated by Annabel, Andrea, or by Lynne and Lindsay, the adoptive parents. There were always meetings at Christmas and birthdays, but in between there would be other informal contact at least once a month.

As Annabel reached seven or eight the contact to some extent diminished, and this seemed to suit the needs of both Annabel and Andrea. Andrea at this point in her life had entered a new relationship and had also begun a new job and Annabel, like many children of her age, was beginning to become much more preoccupied with her own world. There was still regular contact at main events like Christmas and birthdays and mostly phone contact at other times, with occasional informal meeting. Currently, with Annabel in early adolescence, there is an informal relationship, not unlike the 'drop-in' relationships many adolescents favour with their peers, in which contact is mostly negotiated by Annabel and Andrea directly.

Though there is some general acceptance that where children grow up in long-term foster care placements they should maintain links with their original families, social work practice has commonly been to sever any links in adoption or permanent placement. In recent years the question of maintaining links in adoption has begun to be debated in this country (see for example the Adoption Law Review Consultative Document, 1992) but there are many who oppose it as something which is radical and untried, or as having nothing to offer those who are adopted. A good example of such opposition is to be found in the recent Social Services Inspectorate report concerning post adoption services in three northern counties (Dews *et al*, 1993). The report has little positive to say about both post-adoption support and post-adoption contact, and its tone is typified by its criticism of workers in one county who were considering resuming face-to-face contact between a mother and her child who was to be adopted (p. 39, para. 7). It is also very discouraging about even basic post adoption services like a post box service for the exchange of written information (p. 18, para. 40). It is difficult to see from the largely negative tone of this report how it could have been written by anyone who was familiar with the body of research that relates to openness.

Though there is now evidence that maintaining contact between those who are adopted, or otherwise permanently placed and their birth relatives is relatively common in the United Kingdom (see for example Fratter *et al*, 1991; Ryburn, 1994, in preparation), there is greater experience of openness in some other countries. Thus continuing contact between the parties in some form is almost universal in New Zealand. It is also common in many American states. For example, in a major survey involving a random sample of 1,307 adoption placements made in California over a one year period beginning in July 1988, 719 placements involved continuing contact after placement. Openness is promoted by legislation in some Australian states, and one Australian state, Western Australia, has a proposal for new legislation which would alter the whole basis of adoption so that it becomes a "negotiated agreement" between birth families and adoptive families (van Keppel, 1991)[1]. At the heart of the debate about open adoption is the question about what is best for children.

The best interests of children
The best interests of children will always be a relative notion where factors such as age, culture and other individual circumstances have to be considered and judgements made. Nonetheless, the law requires that where children are deemed to be in need of care or protection a view must be taken of *individual* welfare. In doing so it has perhaps lent support to the

---

[1] A form of mediated agreement has also been used successfully in the United States (see Etter, 1993).

idea that the interests of children are readily separable from those of others in their families of origin. The debate about open adoption centres on this proposition. Those who support the idea of continuing contact in adoption between those who are adopted and their original families maintain that to varying degrees the welfare of each of us is linked inextricably with our original families.

The common ground in the debate about what children need has been succinctly summarised by June Thoburn (1993).

All studies of children who are unable to be brought up by their natural parents strongly support the view that two essential elements in enhancing the well-being of such children are a sense of continuity in belonging to a family of which the child feels him or herself fully attached (usually referred to as a sense of permanence) and a sense of identity which is best achieved by continued contact with important people from the past.

It is only recently that a child's need for a sense of permanence has not been seen necessarily to conflict with the need to maintain a sense of continuity in order to achieve a healthy sense of identity. The change in thinking stems from a variety of sources.

The original thesis of Bowlby (1952), concerning the need for a constant mother attachment free from disturbance and interruption, has been modified by Bowlby and others to accommodate more flexible ideas about attachment and bonding. The early studies by Triseliotis (1973) and others concerning the damaging effects of secrecy and lack of information about family of origin on self-identity in adoptees encouraged the beginnings of debate and were influential in persuading the Houghton Committee (1972), as has been noted, to recommend the provisions relating to access to records which were incorporated first in the 1975 Children Act.

The consumer voice represented by groups like NORCAP began clearly to express the wishes of those living with adoption, and the influence of such groups has been very important over the years. So too has the consumer voice represented in such powerful autobiographical accounts as Florence Fisher's *The Search for Anna Fisher* (1975), Betty Jean Lifton's *Twice Born* (1975), and Joss Shawyer's *Death by Adoption* (1979). A growing body of research like that of Winkler and van Keppel (1984), emphasising the sad consequences for birth parents of lack of knowledge and information concerning their adopted children, also played an important role in the debate.

Significant too, throughout the 1980s, was increasing research evidence relating to contact in other forms of substitute care. This highlighted the importance of the maintenance of links for children in care with their original families and emphasised that they could suffer potentially very damaging consequences when these were allowed to wither (see for example Millham *et al*, 1986; Fisher *et al*, 1986; Vernon and Fruin, 1986).

The more open practice of innovative and highly successful placement agencies such as Barnardos in Essex (Fratter, 1989) and Parents for Children (Argent, 1987) showed that open approaches were possible in the context of this country.

Those pressing for better services for black children brought different cultural awareness and perceptions about the nature of family and the capacity of family for what Holman (1980) once described as "inclusive" relationships. Their views injected new thinking in the debate about continuity and permanence. Finally, account began to be taken of experience in other countries, especially New Zealand (see for example Mullender [ed.], 1991) where there was an established history of successful practice in open adoption, and where the twin needs of permanence and continuity could be shown to be compatible.

The origins of secrecy
The origins of secrecy have been discussed elsewhere (see Ryburn, 1994, in preparation). Ultimately it was probably introduced because of the effective lobbying of adoption agencies on behalf of adopters who were anxious to limit both the disclosure of their infertility and to preserve the sanctity of

their family life from "interference" by their children's original families. Secrecy also offered a means to protect adopted children from the substantial stigma that attached to non-marital birth, and therefore, it was argued, enhanced the likelihood of their being adopted. For birth parents it was perhaps seen as offering a new beginning, unencumbered by the past. However, judgements about moral worthiness were such, as Benet (1976, p. 73) records that, in the early years of adoption history more mothers wishing their children adopted were turned away as unsuitable 'stock' by agencies than were accepted.

It took time for secrecy to find support from psychological theory. The idea that the achievement of a sense of security and permanence in adoption is incompatible with the maintenance of contact with original families, could most clearly be abstracted from Bowlby's seminal work for the World Health Organisation (1952). His ideas about the vital importance of undisturbed mother love were of undoubted significance in shaping thinking about the welfare of children, including the need, where adoption had occurred, for an environment that was free from 'interference'.

More recently the idea that past links should be severed in order that children and their new parents make secure attachments to each other is attributable particularly to the work of Goldstein, Freud and Solnit (1973, 1979). These authors went so far as to assert that in situations where children were apart from a parent, by virtue of a marital separation or divorce, only links with the parenting parent should be preserved. Their conclusions were based on their own clinical experience and did not arise from any empirical research. Although their views have no foundation in research much importance is still placed on them by many local authorities and adoption agencies in their child care planning.

Other writers have also argued from theoretical perspectives that the severance of past links was important. Kraft and colleagues (1985, 1986) express the view, based on clinical practice in the psycho-analytic tradition, that the attachment and bonding between a child and adoptive parents requires the security and permanence which can be achieved only through secrecy. They express the view that birth mothers are often too developmentally immature to manage the complexities of open adoption and that their capacity successfully to grieve the adoption will be diminished by contact. They also maintain that adopted people require the protection afforded by secrecy. Arguments of a similar nature, based on clinical experience, are advanced by others such as Byrd (1988) and Foster (1979).

Adopted people
The need for information
Available evidence from both research and practice quite clearly supports the idea that maintaining some form of contact for children and young people in permanent substitute placements (including adoption) can be beneficial.

Early studies about adoption and identity in the United Kingdom by McWhinnie (1967) and Triseliotis (1973), and by others (see for example Sorosky *et al* 1978) indicated that adoption could sometimes be secret from those who were adopted, and that the discovery in adulthood of adoptive status could be a shattering event.

These studies began to highlight for those who were adopted the need for knowledge about their adoptive status and for access to information about their original families, in particular the reasons for their having been adopted. This was seen as important, perhaps essential information, in creating the necessary understanding for identity security. Triseliotis's study (1973) discovered a link between the absence of such information and a degree of confusion about identity.

Certainly adoptees, who seek reunions in adulthood seem primarily engaged in a search for themselves, as this woman described:

That need in me to find her, that searching, was really the hope that I would discover who my true self really was.

(previously unpublished interview with the author, 1987)

When adoptees do meet birth parents they do not often describe their relationship as a parent-child relationship The accounts of the three adoptees below illustrate the different quality that time and circumstances bring to relationships.

It's a funny relationship. You're not really like mother and daughter. You're coming together as two adults really ...

(Rockel and Ryburn, 1988, p. 78)

Your natural parents are part of your life, but in no way will they ever take the place of your adoptive parents.

(Rockel and Ryburn, 1988, p. 77)

I doubt if there will ever be a mother-daughter relationship between mother and I. There's been too much water under the bridge for that ... but there could be two women with a lot in common.

(Rockel and Ryburn, 1988, p. 83)

Multiple attachments
Underlying the original thesis of Goldstein and colleagues was the notion that children would be able to sustain significant attachments with only one parent or set of parent figures. Those who oppose open adoption argue that the maintenance of contact with birth relatives, parents in particular, will create confusion for children and young people and may create conflicts of loyalty.

It is important at the outset to note that birth families do not customarily play any substantive role in the parenting of children in open adoption. Even in the most open adoptions we encountered in our research in New Zealand (Rockel and Ryburn, 1988) there was only occasional alternative care offered at holiday times or by way of baby-sitting. McRoy and her colleagues (1991) are finding a similar pattern in the most open forms of adoption in their study. It is worth observing that this level of alternative care would be customary for many children whether adopted or not.

One criticism that can be made of those who argue that contact can be confusing in open adoption is that they are applying adult thinking to the situations of children. Brodzinsky and his colleagues (1984a, 1984b, 1992) have discussed and demonstrated how children's cognitive understanding of adoption grows very slowly right into adolescence. Children, at least until middle years, are not likely to have the level of sophisticated understanding to confuse the biological role of parent with the social role of parent. Parents, so far as children are concerned, are those who parent them and a variety of studies, including those in divorce, separation and step-parenting, demonstrate an ability on the part of children successfully to manage multiple attachments and even complicated patterns of shared parenting.

Research that predated the work of Goldstein and his colleagues by Schaffer and Emerson (1964), indicated that children are well able to sustain multiple significant attachments in their lives. In the Schaffer and Emerson study some thirty per cent of infants aged two had up to five significant attachments in their lives. One of the important findings of their study was that the children with the greatest number of other significant attachments were also those who enjoyed the *closest* relationships with their mothers. The study also demonstrated that children were capable from the beginnings of social behaviour of forming multiple attachments.

Fox's research (1977) concerning the shared care of Kibbutzim children aged between eight months and two years also demonstrated that the quality of attachment to mothers was not diminished or compromised as a result of their not being the only or even necessarily the primary caregivers. Even the younger children in the study seemed to be able to distinguish between their mothers and other care givers, and whilst they were happy and attached to other carers they reserved their greatest affection for their mothers. Schaffer (1990) writes that:

... however interchangeable ... people may be for certain purposes, they are clearly discriminated between. It seems that even infants already feel themselves to be part of quite a complex social world; there is thus no need to fear that exposure to a range of individuals will produce confusion as to the nature of that world.

(pp. 83 - 84)

Lessons from separation, divorce, step-parenting
The research in divorce, separation and step-parenting is also relevant. It indicates very clearly that the welfare of children and young people is best served by the continuation of a relationship with both sides of the family. This research comes from both sides of the Atlantic and includes some major longitudinal studies. Notable are those of Wallerstein and her colleagues (1980, 1988, 1989), Hetherington (1979, 1988) and Hetherington and colleagues (1979, 1985, 1989). Some of the United Kingdom research of relevance here has been that of Maddox, (1980) and Burgoyne and colleagues, (1984, 1987). All of these studies emphasise the maintenance of continuity as important to the long-term welfare of children. They conclude that the only possible contra-indication so far as continuing contact between children and both parents is concerned is the existence of open hostility and conflict. They highlight sometimes quite acute grief on the part of children where they are not in contact with a parent. It is worth noting that Lund (1984) has indicated that even in some situations of conflict and hostility the benefits of continuing contact outweigh the disadvantages. Though situations of divorce, separation and step-parenting do not directly parallel situations where there is continuing contact in adoption, we would be foolish not to pay heed to a substantial body of related and relevant research.

Original families
Effects of closed adoptions
There is now a considerable body of research to indicate that birth families can suffer more in adoption where there is no contact. An important study in Australia by Winkler and van Keppel (1984), which surveyed 213 mothers who had relinquished children for adoption, found that forty-eight per

cent of them reported an intensified feeling of loss over the period from relinquishment to the time of the research study. For almost three quarters of the sample it had been ten years or more since the relinquishment. Only ten per cent of women reported that they no longer experienced any loss in relation to the adoption. Sachdev (1991) found of a sample of seventy-eight birthmothers that:

a huge majority, (77 per cent) of the sample ... admitted to having 'very frequent' or 'somewhat frequently' thought of the child they relinquished some fourteen years previously with considerable mixed guilt, pain, and loss.

(p. 259)

The prevalence of a sense of loss following adoption has been identified by many others. Sorosky and colleagues (1978) reported in their survey that by far the majority of birth parents wanted to know how their children were faring and would have wished them to know that they still cared for them. Wells, in a recent study (1994, in preparation), reports that almost all of 262 birth mothers surveyed stated that their physical and or emotional health had suffered as a consequence of adoption, and 207 (seventy-nine per cent) cited major disabling effects such as depression, anxiety, and relationship problems.

In our study (Rockel and Ryburn, 1988) the majority of birth parents who had no contact with their children expressed feelings of loss very similar to those in the Winkler and van Keppel study. The following responses were typical:

It broke my heart. I lost my sense of direction, my motivation. I ended up losing a sense of who I was, why I was here. Yeah I lost my way. I lost my sense of what everything was about. I had no sense of purpose, no sense of feeling worthwhile, low self-esteem. I'd lost a piece of myself. There was a piece of me missing.

I've had to fight my feelings all these years, and I've got so good at it that it's hard to let go. And now that I've started grieving I'm scared - there's so much there that still has to come out. I feel as though there's a volcano or a dam there, and that once it goes ....

There's just been a yearning - a terrible yearning. Especially after I'd had children of my marriage. I always wondered what had happened to her, and where she was, and was she happy. And basically the fact that I didn't have her just left a gap - a hollow in my life.

(Rockel and Ryburn, 1988, p. 32)

In their recent study Howe and colleagues (1992) describe "grief, loss, anger and guilt" (p. 123) as common ingredients for many of the birth mothers in their study. They state that:

The life-long impact of the adoption was highlighted in the discussions about subsequent relationships, marriages and children. Feelings about pregnancy or childbirth had often affected sexual relationships, and the knowledge of a previous child had often shadowed a marriage. Having more children could in no way replace the lost child, but mothers had to keep up the pretence that all was now over and forgotten, and they were now content in their new-found respectability.

(Howe *et al*, 1992, p. 126)

Bouchier and her colleagues (1991) in a recent study in Scotland found that 35 of 41 birth mothers who had relinquished children for adoption reported that they thought often, including daily, about their child. There have been close parallels also in American studies (Deykin *et al*, 1984; Watson, 1988). Although no studies have to date included birth fathers or other birth relatives, the evidence from support groups and post-adoption counselling in both this country and elsewhere is that their grief may be no less severe and prolonged. This is an area where there should be further research.

Adoptive parents
Risks to attachment

Adoptive parents have traditionally been seen as the ones with the most to lose from continuing contact in adoption. There was a general consensus amongst earlier writers that they feared that they would lose the affections and loyalty of the children they had adopted were there to be contact. Additionally there has, as has been noted, always been anxiety that there would be interference by birth families in their parenting relationship (Kadushin, 1980; Sachdev, 1984; Sorosky and Pannor, 1978; Tomlin Report, 1925; Triseliotis, 1973).

Available research in fact indicates that there can be significant advantages to adoptive parents in parenting their children where there is openness. Neither is there justification for the traditional view that contact will bring interference and deprive them of continued close attachment to their children.

McRoy and her colleagues (1988), in an intensive small-scale study involving seventeen open adoptions, concluded that there was a positive relationship between openness and the extent to which adoptive parents felt a sense of 'entitlement' to their children. In their study the greater the degree of openness the more comfortable adopters felt with it. In another small but exacting study Belbas (1986) reached a similar conclusion. Bertocci and Schechter (1991), who surveyed twelve research projects which related to adult adoptees who had searched their origins, concluded that in all studies where adoptees had been reunited there was a common finding that relationships with adoptive parents had improved.

Sachdev (1991), concluding a review of two Canadian research studies, one involving a combined total of 300 randomly selected subjects (152 adoptive parents, 53 adoptees, 78 birth mothers, 17 adoption workers), and the other involving 107 adoptees and 50 birth mothers who had managed reunions concludes:

The data from both studies dismiss the adoptive parents' belief that their adopted children are ungrateful if they manifest interest in their birth parents and reject their fear that they

87

will lose affection and allegiance if their children resume contact with birth parents. The studies show that adoptees recognise the significant role that adoptive parents played in their life in providing them with a loving and secure home. They regard them as real parents who nurtured them and with whom the bond is irrevocable and much stronger than with the biological parents.

(p. 261)

The same study found that almost two-thirds of the 107 adoptees felt inhibited during their childhood and adolescence from discussing adoption with their adoptive parents or in expressing any interest in finding their birth relatives. This is a significant finding which should be put alongside disavowals of interest in origins expressed by some adoptees. Expressions of lack of interest in reunion may perhaps be explained in terms of inhibitions in raising the matter. Such inhibitions presumably derive from some sense of loyalty to adopters, in the knowledge or belief by adoptees that their adoptive parents would not wish them to search.

Sachdev concludes his summary of the two studies with the statement:

Clearly, the findings of our two studies point up the fallacies about the fears and apprehensions the members of the adoption triads harbor regarding each other's motives. It seems likely that the inherent suspicions are largely responsible for the historical secrecy that has been the hallmark of adoption practice. Adoption agencies have reinforced these beliefs among the triads partly because of the paucity of research evidence to the contrary, and partly owing to the need for control and monopolization of the service area.

(p. 262)

It would be a mistake, however, to think that adoptive parents automatically fear and do not want openness. It is interesting to note that, in a national survey in 1990 (unpublished) of a random sample of 350 of its members, PPIAS, the support organisation for adoptive parents, found that contrary to popular belief the vast majority of respondents (320) favoured a degree of openness in their adoptions, and in many instances they wished for more contact than they at that time enjoyed. This is due perhaps availability of support and education to these adopters through their organisation, as well as the confidence that has been acquired through the practical experience of being adoptive parents.

In Dominick's study (1988) eighty-eight per cent of adopters expressed satisfaction and positive feelings concerning the contact that they had with birthparents. In a major survey of open adoption which is currently being undertaken in California Berry (1993, p. 252) reports that in 719 adoptions representing state and voluntary agency as well as independent adoptions, where there was contact following placement, adoptive parents "for the most part, are cautiously comfortable with post placement contact". It is important to note that amongst these adopters were some involving "adoptions of children with a history of mistreatment" (p. 252). In my own recent survey (Ryburn, 1994, in preparation) of seventy-four placements which had followed contested adoptions, in forty-two percent of cases (31) there was birth family contact, in twelve per cent (9) there was contact with siblings in other placements, and in nineteen per cent (14) adopters wished for, but were unable to establish birth family contact.

One of the most commonly expressed fears about open adoption is that there will be disruption to the child not only through the maintenance of links but because birth parents will prove unreliable in keeping up the contact. Such unreliability has not been reported as a feature of large-scale studies on openness (see for example Berry, 1993), and in one recent study which specifically addressed this issue in fifty-six open adoptions "100 per cent of the biological parents had kept their agreements" (p. 261) about contact, and adoptive parents were only slightly less reliable with ninety-eight per cent having kept to contact agreements (Etter, 1993, p. 261).

Recruitment of adopters in open adoption

It is often argued by practitioners that it is not possible to find prospective adopters who could contemplate the idea of continuing contact. McRoy has estimated (1991) on the basis of a current national survey of openness that about a quarter of all adoption agencies in the United States participate in open adoption. Research by Berry (1993) and Barth and Berry (1988) would indicate that in some states such as California, openness is more widely practised than this estimate suggests. Fratter and her colleagues (1991) and other researchers such as Borland in Lothian (1991) demonstrate that in reality there are substantial numbers of children in this country growing up with permanent new families and still in contact with original families. In New Zealand Dominick (1988) concludes there is no difficulty in recruiting adopters who wish to maintain links with children's original families, and in fact adoptive parents are probably the most active group in promoting contact (Mullender, 1990).

Joan Fratter (1989) writes in relation to her research on open adoption:

The study demonstrates that adoptive parents who are willing to maintain links or contact after adoption can be found. Agencies in the past may have underestimated their potential for openness because of their own attitudes about the necessity for a "clean break".... Policy and attitudes affected the type of referrals, the likelihood of a child's need for contact being identified and the recruitment and preparation of adopters.

(p. 213)

Etter in her recent American study of 56 open adoptions concluded that:

The danger is that if the agency staff members are not comfortable with openness and fully identified adoptions, they may discourage clients from choosing to develop a relationship that would be extremely satisfying to both adoptive and biological parents.

(1993, p. 265)

Thoburn and her colleagues' study (1986) on placing children in new permanent families found that often children wanted continuing contact and though some new families were interested in encouraging it social workers were opposed to it. Fratter (1989) noted that:

... open adopters could be recruited through specific advertising and through highlighting the importance to a child of family of origin in the course of preparation.

(p. 203)

The recruitment of adopters who are able to take on board the need for continuing contact has been addressed in this country by a number of agencies in addition to Barnardos. For example, Stevenson (1991) talks about the work of the Church of England Children's Society in Tunbridge Wells in this respect. The approach of a New Zealand agency to the recruitment of adopters who would contemplate openness is described in an article by Howell and Ryburn (1987).

There has been no completed research in the United Kingdom to date about public attitudes to open adoption, though a survey is in progress (Ryburn *et al* in preparation). A recent American survey (Rompf, 1993) of 641 members of the public selected through a process of random digital dialling, indicated that "Fifty two per cent of the respondents either strongly or somewhat approved of open adoption. Another twenty per cent of the respondents answered that open adoption should be an option in certain situations" (p. 227). In this survey it is interesting to note that seventy-seven per cent of those surveyed "believed that adoptive parents should help their adopted children search for biological parents thereby opening up what have been closed adoptions" (p. 227); while "86 per cent of the respondents ... thought adoptees would want to find their biological parents" (p. 227).

Infertility and openness
Though there are discussions in the literature in relation to infertility and adoption, based on clinical and practice

experience (see for example Kraft *et al*, 1980; Valentine [ed.], 1987) the research concerning it has been slight. There does seem to be a consensus in the literature that infertility is a major loss that must be grieved so that a resolution is reached if it is not to continue to exert a major negative influence in people's lives (Shapiro, 1982; Menning, 1977). Practice wisdom has long held that successful adopters, (where there is infertility) will be those who have managed successfully the loss that infertility brings (Kirk, 1964, 1981). Where this has not occurred there is a greater likelihood, it is argued, that adopters will not acknowledge the differences that heredity brings to their children, and fail, therefore, adequately to support the emergence of separate self-identity (Sorosky *et al*, 1975; Kirk, 1981).

If this theoretical perspective is accepted, continuing contact between adopters and birth parents may help, where there is infertility, to give tangibility to the loss and help in the acceptance of difference. It may in other words offer a way out of the paradox faced by adopters in being asked to bring up their children in every sense as if they were there own, but at the same time to tell them always that they are not (Stone, 1989). The effect that continuing contact had on Neil in resolving this paradox emerged in the first interview with the family in 1986:

As the contact has gone along I now think of them as being Robin's birth parents more than in the beginning. I probably did think of them as an aunt and uncle role, but I think that as I get into it (contact), I do think of us as the adoptive parents and them as the birth parents, and it just sort of seems very comfortable.

(Morrall and Ryburn, 1986)

McRoy in the study she is conducting with colleagues (1991) quotes a similar view from an adoptive parent:

... my friendship with the birth mother has helped me resolve my own issues around infertility and given me permission to parent.

(p. 108).

Does contact present problems?
Placement stability
Early evidence about contact between adopted children and birth parents seemed at least to indicate that it was not problematic. Raynor (1980) writes in her study which followed adoptees and their adoptive parents in 160 families that :

... where there was personal contact between the adopters and some member of the child's birth family after the legal formalities of adoption had taken place, this did not appear to have caused difficulties for the adoptees.

(p. 89)

Where children as well as adult adoptees are concerned there is growing evidence that the maintenance of some form of contact is, or would have been, beneficial. Rowe and Thoburn's study (1991) of 1,165 children in permanent placements (both adoption and permanent foster care) found, when other variables were held constant, that the maintenance of contact was a protective factor in helping to ensure that placements lasted. Thoburn's 1989 follow-up of the study she undertook with colleagues in 1986 found that where children were placed for adoption without the levels of contact that they wished for there was a greater likelihood these placements would disrupt. Borgman (1982) had found in an American study that children who had significant links were reluctant to join new families where there would not be contact, whilst where there was contact there was not the potential guilt of feeling that a choice had to be made between the two families. The research by Berridge and Cleaver (1987) on foster home breakdown arrived at a similar finding even for short-term placements. Meezan and Shireman in a two-year American study of seventy-two children who went on to various permanent placements said of direct contact, whatever the initial difficulties in establishing it, it "seems critical to enhancing the possibility of good outcomes for all children in foster care, no matter what the permanency planning goal" (p. 22).

This finding that contact can be associated with placement stability is also supported in research by Borland (1991). In this study of 194 permanent placements (both foster care and adoption) there was a comparison made between the 40 placements which had disrupted and a sample of 60 of the placements which had continued. There was no clear evidence that for younger children where contact was maintained it contributed to the stability of placement, but nor was there evidence that it contributed to disruption. Where children were placed from age ten or older, however, seventy-five per cent of those whose placements had not disrupted remained in contact with their original families. On the other hand, only twenty-five per cent of those whose placements had disrupted had maintained such contact.

Wedge and Mantle (1991) arrive at a similar finding in their recent study. They conclude that in adoption there is the need for an even greater revision of practice to encourage contact than in other forms of substitute care:

The evidence suggests that in matters of adoption the position is even more extreme than with children in care generally. Perhaps a much needed conceptual leap is required generally on the part of practitioners, policy makers, researchers, parents and children alike, to accept adoption with access, and even more especially to maintain links with siblings.

(p. 17)

Contact and attachment

There is evidence of more successful attachment to adoptive families where there is the maintenance of contact. Fratter (1989, 1991) has just completed an intensive research project that involved an initial study with a follow-up three-and-a-half years later. The study involved thirty-two children placed in twenty-two different adoptive families. In summarising her research, she concluded that twenty-one of the twenty-two families in the first stage of the study ascribed benefits for their children to the contact with birth relatives. The follow-up study (1991) reported no significant changes. Adoptive parents also described gains for themselves. One reported gain was a belief that they had been helped through contact in developing a closer sense of attachment to their children from the outset. This resulted, they believed, from their detailed understanding of their child's circumstances and the sense of respect that they had gained for their birth parents. In our study in New Zealand, (Rockel and Ryburn 1988) we found very similar views expressed :

Because of the contact that we have and because we know all about them, medical history, cultural background, I'm sure we've been more free in letting them be brought up not like ourselves.

(Rockel and Ryburn, pp. 170-171)

In her study, Dominick (1988) found that only two of the 156 adoptive parents who had contact with birth parents felt that this contact had hindered their attachment to their child Three-quarters of them believed that the contact had enhanced their relationships.

In one part of a larger study, Kelly and McCaulay (1994, in preparation) conducted a longitudinal study of ninteen children in planned permanent foster care. The children were aged between four and eleven years at placement. The children were followed up over a two-year period and the researchers found that most were well attached to their new care givers. The development of these new attachments, however, had not diminished for them the importance of members of their original families. The researchers found that, if there were difficulties associated with the maintenance of contact, this seemed to have derived from the fact that care-givers and professionals had not managed it effectively.

In adulthood, as has been noted, adoptees report a greater sense of closeness and attachment to their adoptive parents when they have been able to re-establish contact with their birth relatives. In a recent study involving 114 adopted people who had managed reunions, the great majority believed not only that this had led to greater self-esteem but that relationships with adoptive parents were closer as a consequence of birth family contact (Campbell *et al*, 1991).

95

Siblings and contact
Dunn (1982, 1983, 1988, 1993) has been one of the major researchers in this country to consider the importance of sibling relationships. She concludes that for many of us, unlike virtually all other relationships, they may well last a life-time, and that for most they remain important even, or perhaps especially even in old age. This is a conclusion supported in other research, and Ross and Milgram (1982), for example, maintain on the basis of their research that there is a special quality to sibling relationships that means their importance endures when all other relationships except parental may diminish or be forgotten.

Iwanek's open adoption study of seventeen open adoptions in New Zealand (1987) highlighted the value for children of being able to meet their birth siblings. Research in relation to children in care also highlights the importance of sibling relationships. In a 1985 study (cited in DOH, 1990) Whitaker and colleagues at the University of York found that children in residential care welcomed being placed with a sibling. It was a source of support, protection and comfort. The same study showed that often where children were separated from siblings this was a traumatic event, and that even where it had happened years before there was often concern and anxiety about their siblings missing them.

Other research in relation to siblings in substitute care supports the importance of the maintenance of sibling ties and relationships. Berridge and Cleaver's study (1987) of 372 foster placements showed that where siblings were separated these placements were more likely to disrupt. Fratter and her colleagues' study (1991) indicated that the placement of siblings together increased the stability of permanent placements significantly. Wedge and Mantle's study (1991) of 160 children in 71 sibling groups came up with the worrying finding that the children in their study placed by local authorities were twice as likely to be separated from siblings as those placed by voluntary agencies:

The importance of siblings to each other is a fact vital to all engaged in child care social work, particularly those engaged in reception into care and placement in substitute families. Wherever practicable, in all social work activity with children and families, sibling relationships should be allowed to take their natural course in recognition of the (sometimes closet) importance of brothers and sisters to each other. When siblings must be separated then there remains a powerful case for ensuring that the links between them are maintained so that in due course, if they so wish, the individuals can re-unite and re-locate themselves and their identity in that culture where there social understanding was begun.

(pp. 83 - 84)

Benefits from continuing contact
Children
Iwanek's study (1987) reported that the children seemed readily to have accepted continuing contact and that they (p. 35) "seemed at ease talking about" their birth parents. Adopting parents in sixteen of the twenty-two families in Fratter's study (1989, 1991) expressed feelings that were either positive or very positive at the first stage of the research about the benefits and advantages to their children of continued contact. The other families had experienced some difficulties though they did not attribute these to the contact. Contact was rather viewed as a factor which added to the *complexity* of the situation. These families were the ones that had adopted older children, and all their children were aged seven and upwards at the time of placement.

It is worth noting that in respect of eighteen children in the study the agencies referring the children for placement predicted that there would be contested proceedings. The fact that contact was believed in the main by adopters to be of benefit in these potentially difficult circumstances is important. Fratter concluded (1989, p. 207) in the first stage of her study that "Adoptive parents in twenty-one of the twenty-two families believed that their children had gained in some ways from (whatever degree of) contact with birth parent(s)."

The views of adopters concerning contact remained largely the same three-and-a-half years later. Children also expressed

97

overall satisfaction at the follow-up stage with the contact they enjoyed. The key gains that they described were in terms of the issues that earlier adult studies describe: a clear idea of the reasons that lay behind their adoptions and of understanding more about themselves. They seemed also to derive a greater sense of security from the fact that the existence of contact symbolised the sanctioning of their placements by their birth families. Joan Fratter concludes her study by observing:

In particular, the experience of agencies which have developed greater openness in adoption and of the adoptive parents in this study, demonstrates that alternatives to the closed adoption model, although more complex for the participants, emotionally and practically, and more demanding of the agency, can enrich the lives of the adopted children, their adoptive parents and their birth relatives.

(1989, p. 215)

There is an interesting parallel here with the major longitudinal study in the United States of Fanshel and Shinn (1978). This covered a wide cross-section of different sorts of placements in substitute care. The authors noted that even though for some children contact might be at times stressful it offered advantages over the situation of a child without contact who is required to achieve a sense of self-worth whilst at the same time coping with what appears as parental abandonment. They concluded that children were more able to manage additional adult figures in their lives, even if this was at times confusing, than to have to cope with their loss.

McRoy and her colleagues in the United States (1988, 1991) are currently engaged in a nation-wide study which is considering the consequences of different degrees of openness for all the parties to adoption. The study is a complex one which recognises that openness exists along a continuum on which they identify five different categories. They note that often adoptions may progress from a stage where there is the disclosure of non-identifying information through to substantial informal contact. This parallels New Zealand experience (Rockel and Ryburn,

1988) and highlights the fact that flexibility and responsiveness to changing circumstances can be important ingredients in the maintenance of contact.

Overall, these researchers report positive advantages to all members of the adoption triangle and conclude that adoption without any contact is the least desirable of the range of possible options. They are also careful to point out that there is no single type of contact that will be right for everyone, and individual circumstances should always be important determinants of levels of contact in each adoption.

Adopters
Where birth parents had consented, adopters reported a reassurance from knowing that their children's placements had been approved by them. The contact offered continuing evidence of that approval. In Dominick's study, some three-quarters of adopters also expressed feelings of reassurance as the result of contact. We found similar views expressed by open adopters:

Openness now means that there aren't any secrets any more. I can just get on with being Sharon's mum, and because of the contact I have with (Sharon's birth mother) Rachael, I know she feels good about me as Sharon's mum too.

(Rockel and Ryburn, p. 171)

Other researchers have reached similar conclusions (see for example McRoy *et al*, 1988; Gross, 1993). With such openness, children also grow up with the knowledge that their adoptions originated in a personal agreement between birth and adoptive parents, and it is reasonable to assume that the guilt described by adoptees in early studies such as Leeding's (1977) and more recent ones like Sachdev's (1991) is not experienced in these circumstances.

Original Families
There is evidence to support the view that opportunities for continuing contact can diminish the sense of loss of birth parents. Field (1991) conducted a survey amongst 444 birth

mothers in New Zealand, 206 of whom had not had personal reunions with a son or daughter, and 238 of whom had been able to do so. The majority of these women had relinquished children between twenty and thirty years before. Using the General Health Questionnaire (GHQ - 28) and a self-esteem rating scale the study did not discover significant differences between the groups in average self-esteem and total GHQ scores. However there were significant differences between the two groups in response to questions concerning recent feelings about adoption events. The group of women who had had reunions with their sons and daughters reported feeling significantly more positive about adoption events in their lives than the pre-reunion group They also reported much higher levels of perceived emotional support in the months prior to the study. Women in the pre-reunion group who had some information about their child had significantly better psychological well-being and reported more positive feelings in relation to adoption than those who had been unsuccessful in gaining any information about the child they had relinquished.

Another New Zealand study was carried out by Dominick for the Department of Social Welfare research unit (1988). It was a comparative interview survey of sixty-five birth mothers and one-hundred-and-fifty-six adoptive parents (equal numbers of women and men). Twenty eight of the birth mothers had had direct contact with the adopting parents and a further eight had contact by way of exchange of letters and photographs. Only fourteen of these mothers, who had relinquished their children between 1980 and 1983, had not received some information by way of photos or letters concerning their child. Of those birth mothers who had had direct contact with the adopting parents, ninety-three per cent reported that they felt that the meeting had helped them to adjust to their child's adoption. They also described feelings of reassurance in knowing their child's new family so that they could picture them in it, and a sense of relief that they need not now worry about them.

In the first stage of Fratter's study (1989) she interviewed adoptive parents regarding their views about the effect that continuing contact had had on the birth parents of their children.

Those who felt able to comment on the effects of openness for birth parents indicated that they believed they had benefited both in terms of greater self-esteem through their continued involvement in the adoption and in terms of coping with their loss. The interviews with birth parents in the follow-up study confirm this picture (Fratter, 1992).

Adoption as the only alternative to reunification

In recent years much British writing has emphasised adoption as the only acceptable alternative for children who cannot live permanently with their original families. This emerges clearly, for example, in the recent report from the Social Services Inspectorate concerning post-adoption services in three northern counties (1993) where forms of care other than placements secured by adoption seem not to be regarded as fully permanent. This is an emphasis of which a number of researchers have been critical (see for example Thoburn, 1985) as was the Social Services Committee of the House of Commons, (*The Short Report*, 1984). The Adoption Law Review Consultation Document, (1992) and the White Paper (1993) also challenge such a perspective. Those who advocate adoption as the preferred form of permanent placement assert that children need the legal security of adoption in order to feel fully part of a new family. This is a view which has limited the options open to children, skewed the decisions of the judiciary, and is not supported by research into planned permanent placements.

Lahti's seven-year follow-up to the original Oregon Project (1982), which aimed to place in permanent placements some 450 children adrift in long term-care, found that a child's sense of belonging was not related to his or her legal status. The major study on permanent placement by June Thoburn and Jane Rowe (Fratter *et al*, 1991) also found that there was no difference in the security of placements for those who were parented permanently in new families by way of foster care compared with those parented permanently by way of adoption.

Fratter's study (1989) concluded that:

The evidence from the study that a child's need for contact does not necessarily conflict with the achievement of permanence and that a secure placement can be offered to children through permanent foster care extends the options which can be considered.

(p. 215)

There was little research evidence about the use of custodianship, and it was probably little used because of the belief that permanent new placements should only be offered by way of adoption. Ironically, an increase in the number of custodianship orders coincided with its disappearance following the implementation of the Children Act 1989 (DoH, 1990). There was, however, one study by Bullard and colleagues (1990) which indicated that custodianship could be a very satisfactory way of meeting the needs and wishes of original parents, new parents and children and of offering permanent placements. The Children Act 1989 provides the possibility for permanency planning by using residence orders and one of the suggestions of the adoption White Paper, as was noted in chapter one, is for a new form of guardianship which would largely parallel custodianship.

Conclusion
The view that children's links with their original families can only be preserved to their detriment in new permanent placements has been an influential idea in child care planning and placement for several decades. As a result many children who have been in public care may have lost such links forever. The research does not support this view, increasingly it demonstrates that permanence and continuity may co-exist successfully. Continuity through contact can bring significant benefits to children and both their new and original families.

Part II: Experiences of openness

Introduction

The final section of this book is concerned with the views of parties to adoption who have experience of openness. It comprises six separate interviews together with a commentary identifying relevant research and issues in relation to practice in open adoption. The dialogue derives from accounts given in video recorded interviews which were part of a six-year follow-up study conducted in 1992.

The original study involving twenty people was undertaken in the latter half of 1986. The participants in the 1986 study were selected from over 80 possible interviewees who at the same time were involved in interviews for a book written by Jenny Rockel and myself (1988), or had been involved in an earlier research study that led to the production of a first video in 1984/85, which was called *Open Adoption* (Ryburn and Howell).

Those chosen for the interviews were carefully selected because of the breadth of experience that they could bring with their very different experiences of openness in adoption.

The first interview is with Lorette who was selected because her personal experience offered a very clear account of the consequences that could follow for birth parents in adoptions without any form of openness. Lorette's adoption experience typified that of the vast majority of birth parents during New Zealand's period of completely closed adoption, which lasted from 1955, when new legislation was passed, until the end of the 1970s when adoption consumers, helped by some professionals, began to insist on more open models of practice. Her experience is also typical of that of many of the 500,000 birth mothers who relinquished children for adoption in England and Wales from 1927. Indeed, the parallels between New Zealand birth parents, such as Lorette, and English birth parents are so striking that the most extensive recent study here on birth parents (Howe et al, 1992) employs quotations from our New Zealand studies.

The second interview in the 1986 study with a birth mother, Sue, and her son Richard, who had been adopted when he was a few months old, centred on their accounts of the effects of adoption on their lives, of their reunion after 34 years and the changes that this had brought in self-perception and self-esteem. It raised many issues about the long term effects of adoption. Sue indicated how the passage of time had not led to a diminution of her grief over the loss of Richard and Richard recounted a sense of unreality about his life as an adopted person until he was able to meet Sue, and both recalled the significant reappraisal of their lives that meeting each other had brought about. Unfortunately, it was not possible to trace Richard and Sue on my return to New Zealand, so they could not be re-interviewed.

The third interview in the 1986 study involved two adopted young adults, Joanne and Chris. They were chosen because they had grown up without any significant knowledge of their origins, but in late adolescence and early adulthood, respectively, had been able, on Chris's initiative to trace their birth families on both maternal and paternal sides. This interview also involved their adoptive parents, Frank and Evelyn, who had much to say of relevance to Kirk's acceptance and rejection of difference thesis (1964, 1981), and the birth mother of Chris, Lorraine, whom she had met first in 1983. Chris and Lorraine highlight in interview many of the issues explored in chapter three in relation to identity-formation. The follow-up interview did not include Lorraine who now lives in Australia, nor did it prove feasible to include Frank and Evelyn.

The fourth interview in 1986 involved Taff and Lois, the adopters of two girls then in their middle years, Catherine and Selina. They were selected because they had actively sought to open up the adoptions of their two daughters, and their interview, which included the older of the two girls Selina

(Catherine was involved in a netball tournament which was more important to her than being interviewed about adoption!), raised many practice issues in relation to the establishment of contact when it has not existed from the outset. On follow-up Lois and Taff discussed with me their very unhappy experience of contact in relation to Selina. Though they gave me a brief statement, they were not willing to be interviewed on video, though they did give permission for me to re-contact them for a future follow-up..

The fifth interview in 1986 was with an adoptive mother, Lynne, and her two adopted children, a girl then of eight years and a boy of thirteen. They were chosen because one of the children, Annabel, had always had some form of contact with her birth mother, whilst her brother Matthew wished to have contact but it had not been possible to trace his mother. The two young people were interviewed together in 1992, and a separate interview was conducted with Lynne and Andrea, the birth mother, of Annabel. By 1992 Matthew had also been able to meet his birth mother, Sue, and at the next follow-up it is hoped that she can be included also in interviews.

The final interview involved Maria and Tom, birth parents of Robin, then aged two-and-a-half and Robin's adopters, Neil and Sarah, together with Sarah's sister Ann, who had a good deal of contact with them all. There had been substantial informal contact between all of them since Robin's adoption at birth, so this interview in a sense brought the openness debate full circle and provided a marked contrast with the secrecy of Lorette's situation. On follow-up, Robin's birth father Tom was in Canada but Maria's new partner, Marc, and their eighteen-month-old daughter, Gina, were present, as well as another child Charlotte aged six, whom Sarah and Neil had subsequently adopted.

The video interviews for reasons of length have been edited from the field tapes. They were all approved by those interviewed, before the final video production, as being an accurate summary of ideas and information presented in interview. Minor changes for ease of reading have occasionally been made in the transcription of interviews from spoken to written language.

The original sense has always been retained. The text of the interviews is italicised. The videos themselves are in use in over one hundred and twenty agencies in the UK as well as in countries as far afield as New Zealand and Australia, the United States, Canada, South Africa, Finland, Ireland, the Netherlands and Sweden.

5 Lorette

Lorette was sixteen when her daughter Mikhaela was born in 1973. Like thousands of young women of her generation she felt she faced little alternative but to consent to adoption. After twelve very unhappy years she finally gained some information about Mikhaela or Kaela as she now likes to be known. Lorette has lived with her partner, Dave, since shortly after the first interview was videoed in 1986 and they have two children, Alistair aged five and Tim aged two.

Interviewer: *Lorette, in 1986 you'd had some limited information about Kaela. You'd had some photographs and some written information provided by her stepfather Dave. What sort of contact have you had since 1986?*

In 1986 Lorette described even the limited information that she was able to obtain about Kaela as filling a huge gap in her life. With the information she had said: "I feel more complete and more whole again ... I am back in balance. I have been out of balance since she has been taken away, since she's gone, because I am a mother without a child. Now I am in balance again, even though I can't parent her, I can see and I know who she is."

Probably the most striking feature of both the 1986 interview with Lorette and the current interview is the extent to which very limited information was sufficient to help her to transform her life. Before she gained any information Lorette described herself (1986) as "just falling apart - crying all the time. I couldn't work, couldn't sleep, couldn't eat, really really really unhappy". As she describes, in the course of this interview, she has had only sparse information over the years since 1986. Though Mikhaela's adoption continues to be an event of major significance in her life, having enough information to at least fill some of the gaps has enabled her to live her life, as she says, in the present rather than in the past.

It is extremely difficult to grieve the loss of a child or young person in adoption in the absence of continuing information, let alone any form of direct contact. The work that has been undertaken by many researchers into bereavement (see for example Parkes, 1972) indicates that learning to live with and successfully manage a bereavement is achieved only after a lengthy process. It is a process at the end of which we are able finally to internalise an image of the dead person which draws together all of their qualities and characteristics. For members of birth families, separated from a relative by way of adoption, without any form of ongoing contact, it is not possible to internalise a satisfying image of their child or young person. They will live every day with the knowledge that their child or young person is constantly growing and changing in ways that they can know nothing of. This issue is raised later in the interview.

Lorette: *Since 1986 I've had contact from David, her adoptive father by mail about once. I've also received information via another social worker who rang him up maybe once or twice, and I think basically that's about it over the last five years. So it's been very limited.*

Interviewer: *So there's been no direct contact between you and Kaela?*

Lorette: *No, none whatsoever.*

Interviewer: *Now is that because you've not sought it or has she not sought it, or has it not been possible to organise that?*

Lorette: *It's been that way because of the fact that the whole contact that I've had has been so difficult that I have felt that I was being very threatening towards her and her family, or disruptive or whatever, if I pursued it any further than what I have already.*

Much of the opposition to continuing contact following adoption is based on the fear of an unwelcome intrusion by one party into the lives of others. This fear, as chapter one has indicated, is part of the historical roots of secrecy in adoption, but also very much a current fear as well (see for example Henderson, 1990; Jennings, 1992). In some seventy interviews conducted for our book study (Rockel and Ryburn, 1988) we discovered a high level of sensitivity on the part of parties to an adoption in wishing not to disrupt, through contact, the lives of others. This is consistent with reports from the Post-Adoption Centre in London (Sawbridge, 1990). It is a theme which emerges in subsequent interviews. It is worth noting, in particular, Joanne and Chris's comments in the interview which follows Lorette's, concerning their wishes as adopted person and birth mother respectively not to intrude in the lives of others, (see chapter six).

It is probably true to say that those who are seeking contact are often so sensitised to the difficult and conflicting emotions it arouses that they wish to be highly protective of the vulnerabilities of others. The desire for reunion almost always derives from a positive motivation to make life more full, whole and complete, not through any malicious intent. Social policy, however, is often shaped by exceptions, consequences we would wish to avoid, rather than by normal responses which we should accept and support. The evidence that there is about adoptees who search confirms the idea that a wish for contact is not unusual, and that contact when it occurs need not be harmful (see for example Corcoran, 1991). So far as searches by birth parents are concerned there is certainly no evidence to support the contention that "... we must keep in mind that many of the birth parents who are incapable of caring for the child they still consider to be theirs, will abuse the right to have access to the child or the adopter's right to privacy" (White, 1991). This comment also ignores the fact that in some senses "the child" will always "be theirs".

Interviewer: *Is Kaela still living with Dave?*

Lorette: *No, the last piece of information I've had which would have been about April of 1991, she had left staying with her*

109

father and she is now living with her original adoptive mother in Hamilton.

Interviewer: *So you're still in the position of not having a lot of information?*

Lorette: *Definitely. No control.*

The point Lorette makes here seems crucial. Access to full and proper information concerning events and circumstances which have played and will play a major part in our lives is essential to establishing a sense of personal control and direction. This can be a major issue for many people who are parties to adoption, and Lorette's comment parallels those made by others during the course of interviews. In particular, it is worth noting Joanne's comment in the next interview where she states, "I think the not knowing didn't give me a base to anchor any security at all".

Interviewer: *And so far as you know Kaela has had many changes in her life since she was adopted?*

Lorette: *Yes, she has had quite a lot.*

Mikhaela's original adoptive parents separated. She went to live with her mother who entered a new relationship which also ended. Mikhaela then continued to live with Dave, her adoptive mother's second partner, until recently, when, as a result of difficulties in that family, she returned again to her adoptive mother. As Lorette noted in the 1986 interview, it is a cruel irony that she felt under considerable pressure at the time of Mikhaela's birth to consent to her adoption in order that Mikhaela could have a stable and happy life. Wells's recent survey of 262 birth mothers, many of whom were of Lorette's generation, has found that 80 per cent felt that they were under pressure to agree a plan for adoption for their child (1994, in preparation). The subsequent discovery for Lorette that Kaela's family life had been anything but stable and secure highlighted for her, the extreme difficulty of making satisfactory predictive judgements about who will or who will not be suitable permanent parents for somebody else's child (see Ryburn,

1990; Cain, 1992; Ryburn, 1992b). With an estimate that four in ten marriages in this country will end in divorce, (Halsey, 1993) and disruption rates in adoption for some age groups at over 40 per cent, (Fratter *et al*, 1991) we must question critically any assumption that adoption inherently offers a more stable and satisfying life for children and young people.

Interviewer: *Talking to you in that last interview in 1986 about the effect the adoption had had on you, you had this to say:*

It had a terrible effect, a really bad effect. It made my life hell for twelve-and-a-half-years. It was a personal hell that I was going through that I could never talk about, and because I couldn't talk about it I thought there was something wrong with me I didn't realise that other people were possibly in the same circumstance and suffering the same way as I was too, because I couldn't share it, so I couldn't have anybody else identify with it.

Lorette still receives some post-adoption support and counselling from a specialist agency, though not the one which had arranged Mikhaela's placement. Had Mikhaela's adoption been arranged differently, with the built-in possibility for continuing contact, then it seems likely Lorette would not have needed the level of support which she has sought.

Agency responses to the requirement under the 1976 Adoption Act to provide services to children and young people who are or are likely to be adopted, to their adoptive or prospective adoptive parents and to their birth families have often been minimal. This may not simply signal lack of commitment or resources, or both. There is a real issue as to whether placing agencies are the most appropriate agencies to provide post-adoption support. The Post-Adoption Centre in London reports (Sawbridge, 1989) that very often parties in adoption find it difficult to return to the agency with whom they were first involved

Interviewer: *Do you still have that feeling of isolation?*

Lorette: *Very much so, it hasn't really changed that much, the isolation side of it really hasn't changed that much, no, not at all, so I agree with what I said back then.*

Support groups and self-help groups can play a crucial role for all parties to adoption. Lorette's comment about isolation can parallel for instance the feelings of adoptive parents who should be encouraged, in preparation groups, to consider sources of potential future support as well as what ongoing agency support they would wish. Foster parents, for example, are sometimes reluctant to adopt because of a fear of lack of agency support post-adoption. As noted above, it can be very hard for adoptive parents to return for help, if things are subsequently difficult, to the same professional agency that had judged them as competent to manage the task of parenting somebody else's child. To return, in this context, can seem an admission of failure. Where group process has been used effectively in the preparation of prospective permanent foster carers or adopters (see for example Howell and Ryburn, 1987; Stevenson, 1991), then these groups can often form an effective basis for a continuing support group. It should be noted, too, that difficulties can sometimes more effectively be raised with peers than with professionals.

Interviewer: *Have other things changed in relation to the way you feel about the whole thing?*

Lorette: *Things have changed with regard to the way I feel. I feel very angry. I've come to terms with the actual adoption side of it, the actual relinquishment side of it. What I'm still finding hard to come to terms with now, and deal with now, is all those wasted years of anguish and pain and hurt and depression and just wasted, wasted years of my life that have gone. I'm very, very angry about it, very angry. It's just like recently I've gone through this grieving process for all the years that I've lost. That need not have happened. OK the adoption happened, I've dealt with that, but not the lost years, definitely not. There must be so many women out there still going through this, still locked in there, having problems and they can't find out what their problems are, and desperately needing help but being mistreated and misdiagnosed. Like with myself, when I was having all those problems, as I said, I was seeing a psychiatrist for it and they were trying to treat me for this problem which just didn't exist. I didn't need Valium, I didn't need medication, I just needed somebody to relate to the fact that I was suffering this through having lost a child. I didn't have a particularly easy time when I was pregnant with Alistair, my oldest one. Towards the end of the pregnancy I started having these terrible nightmares that he was going to be taken away from me and that I was going to go through the whole thing all over again. There was an awful lot of unfinished business with that regard that sort of came up, and it wasn't a particularly happy time.*

Lorette's comments highlight the fact that it is normal for original families to look back with anger on adoption. This anger can most usefully be seen as part of an unresolved grief, not only for the loss of a child, but for what might have been had there been a better process, less social isolation, more support and a greater understanding by others of the effects that adoption can have on the lives of birth parents and other relatives. It is worth emphasising that, though anger is part of grieving, it is important that it is not labelled as a grief reaction in circumstances in which it is a reasonable and legitimate response to poor services.

Lorette's observation, that over many years following Mikhaela's adoption, there was a failure on the part of professional helping services to acknowledge the crucial role that adoption played in her state of unhappiness, seems a crucial one. Proverbial wisdom such as "out of sight out of mind" and "least said soonest mended" has often informed attitudes to original families in adoption. It is not an uncommon experience for members of original families to recount that adoption was not rated as a factor of sufficient significance in their lives when subsequently they have sought professional help.

Like any major loss, adoption can have a recurring and increasing increase in significance for original families at key points in their lives. There are numerous events, like Christmas and birthdays, the birth of another child in the family, a child going to school, a marriage or a death, which can precipitate feelings of loss. Lorette's comments about the effect that Mikhaela's adoption had on her when she later had other children is reminiscent of similar comments in interviews with other birth families, as the following two quotations illustrate:

I have cried on and off over the years - there might have been something on television or something stirred a memory - and I would cry and my children would say "what's the matter?" And I always gave the same answer, "it's because I'm tired." I must have been just about the tiredest mother. But my eldest girl, she knew, right from the word go. She's told me that right from when she was little she knew there was something, you don't hide feelings that easily.

(Rockel and Ryburn, 1988, p. 34)

There's just been a yearning - a terrible yearning. Especially after I had children of my marriage. I always wondered what had happened to her, where she was, was she happy. And basically the fact that I didn't have her just left a gap - a hollow in my life.

(Rockel and Ryburn, 1988, p. 32).

This last quotation parallels the extract which follows from Lorette's interview (in 1986). Below she discusses the extreme difficulty of grieving an unknown loss.

Interviewer: *Something else that you said in 1986 was this, and I wonder whether you would still agree with it?*

News, whether it be good or bad, is better than no news at all because for twelve-and-a-half years I just had questions and questions and questions and maybes, and ifs and buts, and what does she look like, and maybe she's like this and maybe she's not even like me, or maybe she died when she was six months old. Maybe she's happy, maybe she's not happy, maybe she's sick, and I did get some answers and, as you say, some of them weren't

114

good, but my goodness whether the news is good or bad at least it's real and it's hard and it's solid fact.

Interviewer: *I wonder whether you would still agree that news whether it's good or bad is better than no news at all, because for you the contact you've had with Kaela has largely been unsatisfactory and a lot of it's been bad news, the upsets in their life and the changes and so on. Would you still agree about that?*

Lorette: *Oh definitely. Without a doubt. I mean I haven't really ... I've had bits and pieces of information off and on throughout the years but nothing that I could really grasp on to, but what I have had has filled in the great gaps that are there. And unfortunately I'm in a situation where I just have to be grateful for every little piece that I get, whether it is good or bad.*

Many of us may have an inborn reluctance on occasions to discuss difficult or painful issues with others, especially when they are children or young people, who may be more vulnerable than adults. In considering this issue in adoption it is often instructive to reflect on our own responses to bad news which concerns us. One of the most likely examples is where personal health is concerned. Most of us regard information about ourselves and our bodies as being our information as of right. Whether the news were good or bad, it would still be our news. It is important to consider, therefore, if there are any circumstances in which that same principle should not apply to others.

Should adopted people, for example, be excluded from having potentially painful information about aspects of their lives in their original families? Are there ever grounds, for example, for not conveying information if someone was born as the consequence of sexual abuse, incest or rape? While there may well be agreement that such information should be given, we may often put off conveying it on the grounds that now is not the 'right time'. Yet there probably never is a right time to convey such information; it will always potentially be distressing, and reactions to it could never accurately be predicted. The issue to confront may well be whether not telling is a defensive manoeuvre aimed to avoid personal stress and discomfort for the teller, though disguised in the language of protecting someone else.

As a group adoptees have suffered more than most from this sort of 'protection'. Writing about the subject of adoptees discovering difficult information about their personal history, Griffith, himself an adoptee, had this to say:

In my experience of meeting many hundreds of adoption 'consumers' around the world, adopted people conceived by rape or incest do not normally fall apart when they find out, as many professionals fear. They often cope much better than the people who try to help them. Adopted people have a basic coping method when they discover they were conceived in immoral or questionable ways. They say to themselves: "If my birth parents had not done what they did then I would not be here! So I had better face reality. To fully accept myself I must accept my origins".

(Griffith, 1991, p. 157)

A related issue is how should professionals convey difficult aspects of a child or young person's behaviour or personality or background to prospective adopters who, it is hoped, will offer this child a permanent placement? Is it ever justifiable to avoid giving a full and complete picture in the belief that it is better sometimes to withhold certain information, at least initially, so that an attachment forms more easily? The belief that sometimes underpins such action is that when this information is conveyed, subsequently the sense of attachment that has begun to develop more deeply in the absence of full information may then act as a protective device to ensure the continuation of the placement. The question, in other words, is: does the need of a child for a permanent placement ever outweigh the ethical duty to give full and accurate information?

It is not uncommon for prospective adopting parents to be given less than complete information about a child they are proposing to parent. A recent example concerned prospective adopters of a child whose birth parents both had long histories of involvement with mental health services. These adopters were told that both of the children's parents had been diagnosed as schizophrenic, but what they were not told was that research, based on adoption studies (see for example Kety, 1973) indicates more than a 40 per cent correlation between the development of schizophrenia in both parents and its development in their children. The issue is not only one of conveying information, it is also about explaining its full implications.

It would serve us well in all aspects of adoption to follow Lorette's advice, "that news whether it be good or bad is better than no news at all". The issue becomes in these circumstances not one of whether to tell, but when and how best to do so. The work of Brodzinsky and his colleagues (1984a, 1984b, 1992), as was noted earlier, is very useful in helping us to understand the issues in relation to conveying information in an age and developmental context.[1]

Interviewer: *When you talk about Kaela's adoption, you always talk about it in terms of her being taken from you, and I guess in doing that you speak for thousands of birth parents who signed consents to adoption but looking back on it don't feel that it was a choice that they really made.*

Lorette: *That's right. Well it was society's way of dealing with the situation and you went along with it, you went along with it because that's how it was then.*

The fact that Lorette always describes her daughter's adoption in terms of compulsion, even though she signed a consent is significant. It is inappropriate to talk about choice in circumstances where people do not have access to information, to resources and to alternatives. The choices of those who use the services of local authorities are often curtailed by the multiple

---

[1] For summaries of the literature in relation to telling children about adoption, see Brinich (1990), pp. 9 - 10; Steinhauer (1991), pp. 73 - 75.

disadvantage that factors such as poverty and racism bring with them.

Interviewer: *Does it seem like some sort of punishment to you when you look back on it?*

Lorette: *Punishment! Punishment is the big word. If somebody said to me what would you say ... there are three things I could say about adoption from a birth parent's point of view. One is isolation, the second thing is lack of control and the third and final thing is punishment.*

Lorette's summary of her birth parent's perspective on adoption has close parallels with the comments of many members of original families in both adoption by relinquishment and adoption by contested court proceedings. In contested proceedings these feelings of being punished, and of isolation, are almost certainly heightened (see Ryburn, 1994, in preparation). Research relating to the views of birth parents in adoptions by relinquishment very often confirm Lorette's conclusion (Bouchier *et al*, 1991; Dominick, 1988; Field, 1990; Howe *et al,* 1992; Rockel and Ryburn, 1988; Winkler and van Keppel, 1984).

Interviewer: *Lorette, many people have watched the video* Adoption in the 1980s. *There are many birth parents, men and women, some of whom have had children adopted against their wishes, some of whom have relinquished children as you did, who have told me that watching that video of you has been immensely helpful to them. I know some of them have been in direct contact with you and I wondered if there was any final thing you'd want to say about your adoption experience.*

Lorette: *I will never ever feel again in my whole life how I used to feel. Because of the fact that I relinquished that child, she was taken away and part of me was ripped away, there was nothing inside of me on which I could focus my life really. There wasn't that solid foundation upon which the rest of my life could be built, and [with information] as the years have gone by I have become stronger and stronger, my self-esteem has improved no end and I am in control of my life. I know what I want, I know who I am, I know where I'm going, and if I could get up on a soap box and spout all this off to the whole world, I would.*

In other discussions Lorette has attributed the recovery of a sense of equilibrium in her life to three things: access to what has been relatively limited information about her daughter Mikhaela, contact with other birth parents, and access to professional post-adoption services. The crucial part that quite scant information has played in Lorette's life is particularly important.

There is probably no adoption in the United Kingdom today where it would not be possible to make arrangements for limited continuing information to be forwarded to original families, and very often there is scope for much more than this. Department of Health advice in a recent letter to NORCAP (January 1992) was clear that it is within the role of adoption agencies to share such information, and to take an active stance in assisting those who wish to search for relatives. The Adoption Law Review Consultation Document (1992, p. 6) in recommendation 30 offers an endorsement of this position, and the White Paper (1993) also emphasises the information giving role of adoption agencies.

Postscript

Lorette was finally able to establish contact with Mikhaela in May 1992. Mikhaela had been kept in the dark, by her step-adoptive father, of Lorette's deep interest in her, but contact, initially via a post adoption agency, with Cheryll, her adoptive mother, with whom she now again lives, yielded an almost instant response. Within a week of the contact Mikhaela travelled from the North Island to meet Lorette. She indicated that she had always wanted to know about her, and that though she knew that her step-adoptive father had some photos and information she was aware of his attitude towards contact and never felt able to approach him about it. In a letter describing their meeting, Lorette wrote:

What really helped me to break the ice and to get her to relax was the nervous red flush and rash on her neck, which I touched and said 'Oh you don't get that too do you?' After that we were like old mates.

What a strikingly beautiful, together, intelligent young woman she is. I kept finding myself sitting there, mouth open thinking 'Did I really give birth to this lovely person?' You can tell that she and Alistair are related.

I received a letter last week, the first since our contact, and in it she wrote:

I also enjoyed our meeting, it was really fulfilling and it's sort of filled a gap in my life. I wouldn't mind seeing you for longer next time. It may sound weird, but it's neat to know my real family history. Because now I have real ancestors and I now have an idea where I originated from.

6 Chris and Joanne

Chris and Joanne were both adopted by Frank and Evelyn and are sisters by adoption. Chris, the older of the two, is now thirty and Joanne is twenty-eight. They first made contact with their birth families in their late teens with Chris initiating the contact. Since the interview and video in 1986 both have maintained contact with their birth families.

Chris did not reveal in the 1986 video interview that, in addition, to being an adopted person, she gave birth to a daughter, Tammy, when she was seventeen years old, and Tammy was subsequently adopted. Chris is now married to John and they have a daughter, Anna, aged two-and-a-half.

Joanne has had intermittent contact with her birth family since 1986. The years since then have been difficult ones for her. She has now successfully managed a problem of alcohol addiction and is living with another woman, Cheryl.

Only Chris and Joanne participated in this interview, as Chris's birth mother, Lorraine, who was in the original interview, no longer lives in New Zealand and it was not practicable for Frank and Evelyn to travel from the North Island.

Interviewer: *Joanne back in 1986 you said of the contact that you have with your family:*

Sometimes it's just so difficult it would be easier to go back to how things were before, but to still know them, but to be able to go back and not have the complications of running between people and pretending often.

Interviewer: *Do you still feel like that about the contact you have with your birth family?*

Joanne: *Yes I do. I've initiated change in that way for myself now. I've made decisions about the contact that I have and I don't place myself in situations now where somebody doesn't know that I'm either Peter's daughter or Marg's daughter. I think back in 1986 when it was still quite new, having made contact, I felt like I had to be with the family. I think in fact they felt that I had to be there as well, and that they had to be where I was, and so we all kind of juggled things to make it work. Only I have taken that control back now and have made it, I think, quite clear: "I want to be here and be part of the family, but in a way where I am part of the family and not where I'm just somebody's friend from down the road." My father's children still don't know who I am. My mum's all do now and in some ways in my mother's family it's become easier because my grandfather died not long after 1986 and he was the person from that part of the family who wasn't prepared to accept that I was part of the family.*

Joanne's discussion here raises issues concerning the best ways to manage contact in adoption when it has not existed from the outset. Joanne had faced the difficult situation where the wider families of both her birth mother and birth father had not all been aware of her existence. Because of this, and the lack of contact over the years, she faced, in common with others in similar circumstances, a number of issues once contact was established. In the 1986 interview Joanne talked about the difficulty of knowing what role to adopt in relation to her original families and where they should fit in her life. This is something that many adopted people speak about whether or not they have contact, as the following quotation from an adopted person without contact illustrates:

I remember when I was ten or eleven - it became quite an issue for me then. Somebody in the family was doing a family tree, and I felt that I was on that family tree, but I never really belonged there. But I had nowhere to be put if I wasn't there. I didn't belong anywhere which is a very difficult sort of feeling and to an extent I still feel that now.

(Rockel and Ryburn, 1988, p. 51)

Joanne also indicates the fragmenting effect it can have for a time on the lives of those who, in adulthood, first make contact with new families. It is not only a question of accommodating new relationships, and accommodating relationships with people who may not even have been known about, it is a question also of reassessing existing or former relationships. This is also true for birth parents following reunions:

I'd sort of wiped him out of my memory-bank altogether. He hasn't been real to me for twenty years. But meeting Paul has made Steve real again, and it's really odd, but I keep feeling like I'm sixteen again. I don't want or need to see him or anything, but ... God knows! It now seems strange that I actually share a son with that man - that I'm linked like that to somebody I've ignored and put out of my life totally for all these years.

(Rockel and Ryburn, 1988, pp. 98-99)

A further issue which Joanne raises is the difficulty, following reunion, of knowing how to relate in new relationships with the newly acquired roles of daughter, son, parent, brother, sister, grandparent, and so on. This is very clearly expressed in an interview with this young adopted man:

There's no written material you can look up. If you're going wind-surfing you can find out what to do, but when it comes to this you don't know. Should you call her 'Mrs', or 'Ann' or 'Mum'? Should you shake her hand or hug her or give her a little peck on the cheek when she answers the door? And then there's the question of where to meet, and what to wear and what to say. There's no book you can go to and look up what you do when you meet your birth mother.

(Rockel and Ryburn, 1988, p. 73)

The concern this adoptee raises centred on a feeling that is not uncommon at the time of reunion - that of strong attraction between reunited members of original families (see Howe *et al*, 1992; Rockel and Ryburn, 1988). This may often be to a brother or sister, but sometimes to a birth parent. There is a strong desire to touch the other person. Even the wish sometimes to become sexually involved is not unusual. This is not surprising because in our culture sexual feelings are often associated with a sudden and intense response to another adult. The wish for skin contact may also be linked with the wish to be physically bonded with the birth family - to bridge the gap of the years without contact:

The thing about meeting him that I was totally unprepared for was wanting to touch him all the time. I feel as though I can't control those feelings, yet I have to. I wasn't prepared for that at all. And for a while I even started lactating, which really freaked me out. There's a sense that I want to breastfeed him - to do all the things I didn't do with him. Which society would see as really sick.

(Rockel and Ryburn, 1988, p. 92)

Not surprisingly, it is extremely difficult to manage the powerful and mixed emotions that are evoked in situations such as these. Since adoption does not extinguish the prohibited bounds of consanguinity in terms of the Sexual Offences Act, those who do become sexually involved face the additional guilt and anxiety of knowing, often, that they are committing incest.

Obviously, it helps where people are in touch with post-adoption services if they are prepared for the possibility of these feelings in the early stages of the reunion. Similarly, it helps if they are in contact with others who can encourage them to discuss these feelings should they occur, and support them in managing them. Where possibilities exist for continuing contact from the outset of an adoption, it seems much less likely that such powerful attractions will occur in the same way or be problematic. As the quotations indicate, it is the dislocations in relationships that occur through the absence of contact that create situations in which there is no defined context for two people, intimately related strangers, to begin a relationship.

We'd go out dancing together, and it's just so beautiful. I actually thought I would faint when he got me up to dance the first night because it took me right back forty years to how it all started. I had danced with his father, and I never thought I would dance with my son.

(Rockel and Ryburn, 1988, p. 98)

Interviewer: *Have you ever felt an overwhelming wish to go up to children on your father's side of the family and say, "Look I'm here, I'm your sister", or if not why have you held back from that?*

Joanne: *I think in part I've held back for his sake. I mean I had an incident where I was in Taupo visiting my mother and his parents walked past me in the street and I'd seen photographs of them, and at that stage I hadn't met my mother's parents either; and it was kind of strange standing there seeing my grandparents walk past me and wondering, well, do I go up and say, "Excuse me, you know. I'm ...." and in part I guess it's that sense of protecting their lives as well, not wanting to intrude, or a sense of, well, I don't really belong there, or do I?*

Joanne's comments about her grandparents serve as a useful reminder that when original families are lost through adoption without contact, many others, in addition to adopted people and their birth parents, may be involved. In England there is, for example, an organisation for grandparents (The UK Grandparents' Federation) who have lost children through adoption.

Joanne also returns here to the theme of protection and indicates that her not making contact with her grandparents, when she saw them, derived from a wish to protect both their lives and her own. She suggests two explanations for her wish to protect. On the one hand she does not wish to intrude into their lives, but on the other there is a fear of being rejected should she approach them and ending up feeling she does not, as she puts it, 'really belong there'.

Interviewer: *So you watched them go past?*

Joanne: *Yes. That's the only time I've ever seen them in person. I'm sad about that, partly because in my adoptive family I only had one grandmother and she was much older and I never felt very close to her. There's always been a sense in me of wanting to have grandparents, of wondering what would it be like to have grandparents.*

The fact of adoption can add a dimension to ordinary things. It is not uncommon for children and young people to have lost one or more grandparents, though it may be more common in adoptive families where parents can often be appreciably older than the birth parents. In Joanne's case it seems, however, that the fact of being an adopted person gives a different emotional quality to not having a full set of grandparents in her adoptive family. Adoption, in other words, in circumstances where there is not continuing contact and exchange of information, may provide a context, as the chapter three on identity formation has noted, in which ordinary life events can assume different or greater significance than they would otherwise do.

Lynne, an adoptive mother (see chapter nine), offers a reminder of how unhelpful it can be to imbue events with a particular meaning because 'there happens to be an adoption'. In doing so the essential ordinariness of events may be overlooked, and our reactions and behaviours may correspondingly be skewed.

Interviewer: *Chris, in 1986 talking about the contact that you'd had with Lorraine and your original family, you said:*

It filled in those gaps that I had in my family picture and so that sense of security in me knowing who I am and what's out there, has made me more secure I think in my relationship with Mum and Dad.

Interviewer: *Do you still feel that sense of security with your parents and do you still attribute some of that security to the fact that you have been able to have a good relationship with your original family?*

Chris: *That's absolutely true. I think it's made some changes for me though now. The security with mum and dad is still there, there's no question of that, but in terms of my genetic identity with them, that's changed. I don't feel that kind of security there. Maybe it doesn't make sense, but for instance I was always really interested in my adoptive parents' family tree and all of that. I owned that for myself, but as I get older I don't. And I know how important it is for mum and dad that Joanne and I carry that on, and now my daughter, Anna, and part of me can't solve that really. And I have no information really about my birth family genealogy. It's very difficult to pin them down and get that stuff, and I'll never get it in the way that I can get it from my adoptive parents. But it just doesn't fit.*

Interviewer: *Do they understand how you feel about their history not being your history?*

Chris: *No. No, I think they worry. I think they've picked up a note of hesitancy in me of late. At Christmas time mum said to me, "you do want to know this don't you, it is important to you?" It **is** important to me because it's about them, but it's not important for me because it's not me, if that makes sense. And I can't make it Anna's history either because it's not her history. So it's kind of like our family tree ends with us. I take on my genetic history, I have to. I can't take hold of theirs. I mean I will always keep hold of it, it will always be there, but it's not for me. I would be doing it for them rather than for myself.*

Chris usefully raises a number of issues here. In the interview in 1986 she highlighted the crucial role that contact and full access to information played in helping her to feel more secure in her relationship with Frank and Evelyn, her parents by adoption. Over the intervening six years her analysis of the role that contact and information has played has changed. Though she is still just as clear that contact and information have enhanced the security of her relationship with Frank and Evelyn, she highlights the fact that it has now also heightened a sense of her own different genetic inheritance. Her loyalty on the other hand to her adoptive parents is obvious. It is a loyalty which can be a factor for many adopted people in influencing whether they feel able to discuss adoption with their adoptive parents. It may also influence whether they have contact with their birth families during the lifetimes of their adoptive parents, and, if they do, the nature of such contact (Sachdev, 1991).

It is possible also to gain a sense from this section of the interview, that Chris's heightened awareness of genetic difference has led to a more integrated sense of personal identity. Though she does not say so, having and parenting her daughter, Anna, may have highlighted the differences between genetic and adoptive identity. This is certainly something that other adopted people recount in interviews:

I think the strongest feelings started to come out when I had my own children and watched them grow up. There would be things I saw them doing that were obviously inherited from me, and I found that intriguing. For the first time in my life I could see a direct inherited link with a person, and I had never seen that before. It suddenly dawned on me why people got enthusiastic about seeing inherited traits in children, and it was a whole new awakening - a whole new experience I had never had before.

(Rockel and Ryburn, 1988, p. 48)

The importance for adoptive parents of developing and building on this sense of difference in order most effectively to parent their children was highlighted many years ago by the Canadian adoption theorist and researcher, David Kirk (1964, 1981). The fact that it is something that should also be built on and acknowledged for people who are adopted, as Chris indicates, has received much less emphasis.

Both Chris and Joanne enjoy good relationships with their adoptive parents. It is important to challenge an idea stemming from early research of adoptees which has suggested that those who searched in adulthood were also those who were most unhappy in their adoptive families (see for example Triseliotis, 1973). However, what the early studies, which linked searching with unhappy home life insufficiently regarded is the extent, as Sachdev (1991) has shown, to which guilt may operate for adult adoptees who wish to search. Such guilt is linked with the idea that to search is both a sign of ingratitude and disloyalty. The only means to avoid such a label, where this is perceived by adoptees to be a prevalent social attitude (especially likely to be the case in the social climate of some of the earlier studies), would be to justify searching by describing the unhappiness of home life in the adoptive family.

How much this social construction of the meaning of searching has influenced research findings, by encouraging adoptees to report instead their searches in terms of some deficiency in adoptive family life, it is difficult to say, but this is a factor which should not be overlooked. In New Zealand where it is now estimated that approximately 40 per cent of adult people adopted in stranger adoptions have identifying information (Griffith, 1991) social acceptance of the normality of searching means that we know that " ... most adopted people who search are normal, well adjusted adults" whose search is for "... personal truth, integrity and social identity" (Griffith, 1991, p. 157).

Interviewer: *What about you, Joanne, do you have any of those feelings about Frank and Evelyn's history not being your history, or do you feel differently from Chris?*

Joanne: *No, I feel very much the same way. Particularly so because my mother is Maori although I'd never been told that until we met. But I did find out at that time that Frank always knew, and when I asked him why he hadn't told me he said that he didn't see any reason to and that he would have told me when I came to have children. And so it has been really important for me, actually claiming this, which has meant I've had to let go [of her adoptive family history], and I've chosen to. And I never felt particularly close to them in that way. Like a strong Polish background on Mum's side and a Scottish one on Dad's side, they never felt right, they never sat with me. Like Chris was saying, I'm interested in them because it's them, it's where they come from, it's important to them, but I certainly don't feel connected to it and that I continue it. And there **is** a conflict, you know. I found a conflict with Mum and Dad about me talking more about* *me being Maori. It quite blatantly conflicts, I guess, with their Polish and Scottish ancestry.*

Interviewer: *Well it makes you very different.*

Joanne: *Yes.*

Joanne's discovery of her Maori identity she describes as an event of great importance to her development of self-identity. She describes, with what seems like a measure of relief, being able to let go of her adoptive parents' cultural and ethnic identities, which she says never seemed as if they fitted for her, despite the fact that as she grew up she had no knowledge of any other background. This is something reflected by other adopted people. The following quotation is illustrative:

My adoptive parents were very proud of their Scottish ancestry, and I was brought up as part of that ... and I do remember wondering sometimes whether I really belonged. Not knowing what blood I had in me, whether I was Scottish, Norwegian, or French. Wanting to belong, but feeling deep down that perhaps I was an impostor. It felt like being a member of a club and not knowing if I was actually qualified to join.

(Rockel and Ryburn, 1988, p. 51)

The fact that Frank, if not Evelyn, had always known about Joanne's Maori ancestry, and the difficulty that they have, despite the closeness of their relationship, in talking with her about being Maori, highlight how difficult identity issues sometimes can be for adoptive parents. To be able to acknowledge the birth inheritance of adopted children when there is no continuing contact and information sharing can potentially make this more difficult.

Interviewer: *One of the things I recall quite vividly that you said in 1986 was that as children you really didn't talk much about being adopted because you felt that in some sort of way that would mean that you aren't sisters. Now you are both becoming increasingly aware of your genetic inheritance, which is obviously very different, has that altered the way you feel about each other as sisters?*

Chris: *I think our relationship is much better than it was (laughter).*

Joanne: *Yes.*

Chris: *... because we are acknowledging the differences now. Like Jo's my sister. My birth sister isn't my sister in the way that Jo is and never will be.*

Chris's observation that differences need not be avoided and that the acceptance of difference can create closeness in relationships rather than distance, is perhaps an antidote to the view that intimacy in relationships depends on the mutual creation of similarities. This is a theme upon which Gregory Bateson, (1980) elaborates in what he described as the two polarities of complementarity and symmetry. Both exist in different proportions in each relationship, he maintains.

Interviewer: *Joanne, another thing I recall your saying [in 1986], talking about when you first met your birth mother, was this:*

It was difficult in that all of a sudden she was a real person and so I had to let go of all the sort of ideals I had about what my mother would be like. You know I had this picture of her, she'd be this all-perfect woman, and then there she was, so it was hard to just come to grips with her being a person.

Interviewer: *Have you come to grips with who your birth family is as 'real' people, to use your word.*

Joanne: *In some ways I have. There's still a lot I feel I don't know about them, and about the people they are. I'm much more willing to accept them these days for who they are. Certainly the glamour and image of this perfect woman and this perfect man living perfect lives has gone, that's certainly not the reality, and I'm glad it's gone as well. It was a bit like you know when*

131

you're kids, everybody else's mother you want as your own mother and your own one's not good enough, and it was a bit like that, you know how I imagined it would be. I'm certainly glad now that the reality is as it is, that I don't have all those expectations. I think in part for the first couple of years of contact I tried to maintain those expectations. You know I only saw what I wanted to see. It's meant as I've got to know them more and as they've got to know me more, we've probably moved apart through contact, but at least it's more real.

There is a sense of reality that contact alone can give to the relationships of adopted people with their original families. Where contact is only established in adulthood it may take a long time before adopted people are able to gain a realistic appreciation of their original families. Even after ten years, Joanne describes the feeling there is "still a lot I don't know about them and about the people they are".

Adopted people have a relationship with their original families, whether or not they are in contact with them. The difference that contact can make is in terms of whether this is a relationship shaped by imagination or one which is grounded in experience. Joanne described graphically in 1986 how contact finally helped her to let go of all the images that she had of what her mother would be like. The reality has not always been very satisfying and for a time during the initial period of contact she describes wanting to try to live out her fantasy images rather than the real ones. She concludes that, even if sustained contact has gradually led perhaps to greater distance in relationships, at least it is a relief to enjoy a relationship focused in reality.

Interviewer: *Joanne, you've talked about the importance of your birth inheritance for you, but certainly all of the things in your birth inheritance have by no means been good things. I wonder whether you ever feel angry also about what you've inherited from your birth family?*

Joanne: *I don't think I feel particularly angry about it. The alcohol addiction is certainly in the past. When I look at the family now it was something that was going to happen to me probably regardless. But the other part of it for me was, I think, in some ways related to me being adopted and not knowing who I was, and it was a search for that.*

Interviewer: *Do you think that adoption, the fact of being an adopted person, held you back in establishing your own adult identify and clarifying your own sexuality?*

Joanne: *Yes, I don't think I grew up until I was twenty-five, twenty-four or twenty-five and I think I was only able to do that, because I had some information then about my birth family and I could start to put the pieces together. It gave me a base to grow up on which I don't think I had before. I think the not knowing didn't give me a base to anchor any security at all. And certainly, now, finding out gave me some information about who I was and therefore what I wanted to do and where I wanted to go.*

The information that Joanne describes as being essential to her ability to 'grow up' was not information that could have been conveyed readily in written form. It was too detailed, too subtle and too complex for such description. If a comparison is made of the 1986 video tape interview with Joanne and the current one Joanne appears to provide clear visual evidence of her statement that she has now been able to put the pieces together in her life, in that she presents as a much more confident person who is at ease with herself in a way that she did not seem to be in 1986.

It is worth noting that a number of studies in adoption do show a significant correlation between alcohol addiction in birth parents and their adopted sons or daughters (Goodwin *et al*, 1974; Cadoret and Gath; 1978; Bohman, 1978).

Interviewer: *Chris, for a long time you didn't feel able to talk openly to many people about the fact that you were a birth mother. What brought about the change, and made it possible for you to be open about it?*

Chris: *I don't think I had any choices about that. I had to start looking at the problem because I put it away and the pain of it was still, is still, there, but it was destroying me I think, slowly. Destroying the way I worked, my relationship, and I think probably around the time that I became pregnant with Anna, I suddenly realised that if having a second child was going to be different, I had to do something about it.*

Interviewer: *What sort of contact and information do you have concerning Tammy?*

Chris: *I wish I could say I had a really good open adoption as far as Tammy was concerned. I don't. I've had a relationship with Tammy's parents which has really fluctuated. They have made offers to me and then not felt able to come to the party really, and so I've had that kind of building up and then being let down over a number of years now, probably ten years.*

There is an interesting parallel here with Lorette. In both instances it seems likely that having second children highlighted many of the issues. Birth parents who have had children adopted against their wishes also describe how the birth of a subsequent child can provoke great emotional turmoil, heightened in their case by the fear that this child also may be removed against their wishes and placed for adoption (Ryburn, 1992b, 1994, in preparation).

Chris's comment that the adoptive parents of her first daughter Tammy have made offers to her and then not "felt able to come to the party" contrasts with the fears often expressed by professionals, and sometimes by adoptive parents. These are fears that the original families of children or young people who are adopted may prove unreliable and that there could, as a result, be acute disappointment for the children involved. Chris's experience with the adoptive parents of her daughter is a reminder that we are all capable of unreliability and letting others down when we are afraid of being hurt. It highlights the importance of adequate preparation for contact in adoption so that there is a negotiated agreement at the outset which can accommodate future changes. Research indicates that, where there are clearly negotiated agreements about contact, the birth parents and adoptive parents are able to maintain them, (Etter, 1993).

Chris's comment, and those of Matthew and Annabel in chapter eight, highlight the lack of pressure and stress which attaches to contact with their birth mothers. Where contact develops as a disproportionately significant event, rather than an ordinary occurrence, there is inevitably much greater scope for fear, disappointment and potentially for things to go wrong. Experience seems to indicate that where contact is most successful it is because it is something that has been successfully integrated in the lives of the various parties.

Interviewer: *What stopped you from going there and tentatively, but in a much more sort of direct way, saying ...*

Chris: *I've attempted to do that, not myself but through a third party. They don't want to know and the only way I could do it would be to turn up on their doorstep, and there's no way that I'm going to do that. I don't want to intrude upon their lives, it's not what I want, I just want, I want to know how she is and how she's doing. Photos don't tell me that, they don't tell me anything. They give me a glimpse of her life and that's it, but that's all I've got at the moment. That's all I can have until she's of an age where she's able to make the decision for herself really, and I have to accept that.*

Chris here returns to the theme of protectiveness, and is clear that she does not want to intrude in other people's lives. She wants to know how her daughter, Tammy, is and what sorts of things she is doing. Her comment that photographs do not convey this sort of information, except by offering a tiny glimpse of life, raises issues about the various forms of possible contact. Though any information can seem better than no information, letters and photographs seldom give the level of detail that makes another person 'real'.

Chris ends her statement by looking forward to a time when Tammy is old enough to be able to make a decision herself about contact. If her decision is to establish direct contact with her mother, then Chris will still no doubt have to live with the sort of anger and grief that Lorette expresses for all the 'lost years'. Chris highlights what should reasonably be an aim for all contact in adoption: creating possibilities for adopted children and young people to express clearly the sort of contact that they themselves would wish for, and working towards it. This is an aim that is now clearly expressed in the Children Act 1989 in relation to other areas of child care.

Interviewer: *Frank and Evelyn aren't here today but if they were what do you imagine they would say about all of your lives in adoption over the past six years?*

Joanne: *I think Dad would say, "We just get on with it. We're all grown-ups now, we're just still getting on with it". Partly, you know, I've thought that over the last few years in some ways they may have come more to terms with adoption themselves. That's my sense, and in some ways they don't take so much responsibility for everything that's happened in my life and everything that's happened in Chris's life. They seem to have let go a little bit from us being their flesh and blood.*

Many adoptive parents talk about feeling an extra sense of responsibility in parenting children that were not born to them. The acknowledgement of genetic difference, which can be assisted by continuing contact, perhaps helps adoptive parents, as Joanne suggests, to let go of the burden of an unnecessary sense of responsibility. In doing so they may permit their children to be more free to develop their own identities.

Chris: *I think they also see us as adults now, far more than they ever did, even in 1986. I mean we've finally grown up, which probably isn't unusual for lots of families, but maybe, I don't know, the adoption thing added another dynamic to it.*

Interviewer: *You mean adopted people ...?*

Chris: *Don't grow up so fast in other people's eyes, they're always adopted children.*

Interviewer: *Right. And they're children for whom other people make the ...*

Chris: *The decisions.*

Joanne: *Yes.*

Chris expresses the belief that being adopted can mean being treated like a child, even in adulthood. This is a view expressed by other adopted people (see for example Bertocci and Schechter, 1991) and probably reflects the extent to which adoptees can feel that key decisions in their lives have been taken by others, sometimes in ways that permit none of the scope for negotiation that many who are not adopted may take for granted.

7 Lois, Taff and Selina

Lois and Taff adopted their two children, Selina and Catherine, in infancy and they grew up always knowing that they were adopted. Both girls are now in their late teens. Lois and Taff decided to establish contact with the birth families of each of them before they reached the potentially difficult years of adolescence. They felt the lack of contact would be an added difficulty at that time. They established contact with their daughters' birth families independently of Selina and Catherine when the girls were twelve and nine respectively.

Having established a relationship themselves, they subsequently introduced their daughters to their original families. Catherine's open adoption has continued, since this time, to work successfully for everyone. However, about two years after they were interviewed in 1986, when Selina was fourteen, she went for a year to live with her birth mother. The original family sought to use a provision of the New Zealand Guardianship Act, whereby with leave of the court any person can apply for custody and guardianship of a child, regardless of whether they are adopted or not, on the grounds that this would best serve the interests of that child. Before the court dealt with the application Selina elected to return to Lois and Taff. There is no doubt that Lois and Taff had not the slightest sense of the way that Selina's adoption would develop when the three of them were interviewed in 1986.

Though it was not possible to re-interview Lois and Taff the material which they provided, together with their interview in 1986, is extremely important since it touches on the fears that many people, in particular adoptive parents, may have about continuing contact in adoption or about open adoption.

It is important to note that Lois and Taff had two adoptions in which there had been no contact from the time of placement, although some information had been made available to them concerning both their daughters' original families. Their decision to seek to establish contact with the girls' birth families came as a consequence of what they described in 1986 as their inability to meet the girls' growing needs for knowledge and understanding concerning their families of origin.

In 1986 Lois and Taff expressed the view that the difficulties for their daughters of managing adolescence should not be compounded either by the lack of such knowledge and understanding or by having, at that stage in their lives, to deal with the establishment of contact. It is true that adolescence is often a difficult period for young people, one in which, as Erikson, (1980) and many others have highlighted, issues of personal identity can be to the fore. Whether there is a right age for children to establish contact when it does not already exist is probably impossible to say with certainty. Lois and Taff's view that it should be before adolescence and as early as possible finds support from Matthew and Annabel in the next interview (see chapter eight).

It is perhaps significant that it is the younger of the two girls who has most easily managed contact, but there are a host of other factors, including temperament, that could influence this. The research does indicate (see for example Schaffer, 1991) that children are able to manage multiple relationships from an early age, and as Lynne, an adoptive parent with experience of early contact for one child but with contact only at the beginning of adolescence for another, remarks in a subsequent interview (see chapter nine), "children are incredibly accepting when they're young and it's a lot easier." It is also important to note that the disruption of adoption placements is not particularly unusual. In a number of studies in this country for instance, the disruption rate over all ages is over 20% (see for example Fratter *et al*, 1991).

One of the significant factors to take into account in the way that contact was established for Selina and Catherine is how it was initiated. In this particular instance Lois and Taff were able to establish, as they described in 1986, "contact with the birth mothers and their families of both their daughters". They had appreciable contact without any involvement of Selina and Catherine until they reached a point at which they felt confident that the contact would work out. It was only then that they introduced their daughters to their original families. They recounted, in 1986, an intense period of several days during the Easter when they first shared all the information they had gathered with the girls, and then introduced them to their birth mothers and their wider families.

There is not the opportunity to have more than one attempt to manage first contact in circumstances such as these. Lois and Taff believed that it was appropriate for them first to feel a degree of assurance about the potential for future relationships between them, their girls, and their original families, before they all met. With hindsight it may be that they would now wish to have managed the contact differently. As Chris emphasises (see chapter six), children and young people who are adopted (as well as young people who are in the public care system) often feel that they have an insufficient say in the key decisions in their lives.

It would have been helpful to talk with Selina, but we could speculate that as she approached adolescence, with issues of control and independence to the fore, she came to be resentful of the fact that contact had initially been established with her mother and her original family without her knowledge, approval and participation. Certainly, as Chris remarks, (see chapter six), issues of control over life decisions can assume an extra dimension for adoptees.

That Lois and Taff were unable to predict the way that the contact with Selina and her original family would develop should not be seen as indicative of a lack of perception on their part. If we compare Lois and Taff's lack of accurate predictive ability with much of the research about outcomes for children and young people in the care system, where the decisions have been made following assessment by professionals, we find that very often professionals show a similar inability to predict accurately. We can look at the high proportion of children and young people in the care system who suffer unplanned and premature ends to their placements in substitute care, even though this same care was assessed as suitable and appropriate (Vernon and Fruin, 1986; Fisher *et al*, 1986). Lois and Taff's inability to see that Selina's future relationship with her original family might not turn out as they themselves wished is reflective of an inability in all of us to manage life with any substantial degree of predictability.

The following extract from the interview in 1986 gives a flavour of the contact between Selina and her birth family at that time.

Interviewer: *One of the things you discovered was that you don't just meet a birth mother you actually meet a whole new family.*

Lois: *Yes, initially you are probably only thinking about a birth mother but it doesn't stop at that, it goes right out, and Selina's really lucky 'cause she's got aunties and an uncle and she's got a nanna, a birth nanna who just absolutely loves her, and that's really terrific because now she's got three nannas that love her not two.*

Interviewer: *Do you get extra treats by having so many nannas?*

Selina: *Yes (laughter)*

Taff: *I think it would be impossible to meet a birth mother and then just leave it at that because the birth mother's family want to know about us. They want to meet us, they're interested in where we live, how we live, who our friends are, and I think it would be a wee bit selfish to meet the birth mother and then send her away again.*

Interviewer: *Taff do you ever think that it could be confusing for Catherine and Selina to grow up having contact with their birth families as well?*

Taff: *It's never occurred to me as confusing, maybe more complicated. I don't think it's a thing that does confuse children,*

141

children will accept established relationships the way they are. That's why we haven't felt threatened at all because we are well established here, as their mother and father in our house.

Interviewer: *I can imagine a lot of people saying, "aren't you frightened that you are going to lose your children, that they are going to want to go back and be a part of their birth families again?" How do you feel about that?*

Lois: *Well you're quite right there, we've had lots and lot of people who have said that very thing to us, "aren't you afraid that they will want to go back?", but the answer has always been emphatically no, we don't feel threatened in any way, never ever have we felt threatened. Because Selina's birth mother and our other daughter's birth mother have in the meantime got on with their own lives and they are happy, and now of course they are even happier after what has happened. But they are happy to continue the way they are and be part of our extended family, and we don't feel threatened. Not at all.*

With hindsight there is perhaps an indication of the difficulties that Lois and Taff may encounter in respect of Selina's family when they talked about their relationship in terms of her original family being incorporated into their family. There is a lack of any sense of reciprocity in the way that this is discussed. Andrea, birth mother of an adopted daughter (see chapter nine) agrees, in contrast, that the adoptive family of her birth daughter, Annabel, has to some considerable extent been incorporated into her own family, just as she is in theirs.

Original families both in adoptions which are relinquishments, and adoptions without consent, often describe feeling that they seem to be regarded as nothing more than a source of information for identity purposes so far as their adopted children are concerned (see Ryburn, 1994, in preparation). It is not suggested that this is how Lois and Taff regarded their daughters' birth families, but it is clear that the expectation was one primarily of the original families accommodating themselves to the girls' adoptive family. This is an approach that seems more likely to work during the period of first contact, when birth parents are likely to feel very grateful to the adoptive parents for their willingness to offer them contact. As time goes on, however, it would doubtless not be unusual for birth parents to wish a greater degree of reciprocity than this, and perhaps this began to happen with Selina's birth family. Contact without any great sense of mutuality is also more likely to be unproblematic where there is a single birth relative relating to an adoptive *family*. In Selina's case, much more than Catherine's, there was an extended family network of people who wanted contact and possibly had a collective wish for a more reciprocal relationship than they were able to enjoy. Perhaps this contributed to a possible failure on their part to respond as helpfully as they might when tensions began to develop for Selina with her adoptive parents Lois and Taff.

It is important to note that Lois and Taff acknowledge Catherine's open adoption is going well and is satisfying to her, and that Selina of her own volition elected to return to her adoptive family. From Selina's perspective we could speculate that from a future standpoint the time which she was able to have with her original family was very important in helping her to establish her sense of identity and gain a much fuller appreciation of her place both in her family of origin and her adoptive family.

When contacted, Lois and Taff were not prepared to be interviewed again. They stated that the years since 1986 had been a time of such turmoil in their relationship with Selina and her birth family that they did not feel emotionally resilient enough to discuss it. Lois did however prepare a brief statement which Taff indicated also represented accurately his own views. It follows below:

I still believe it is the right of every adoptee to knowledge of their birth families. However opening up the adoption of our elder daughter Selina completed destroyed what had been a close family unit. It resulted in a five-month court battle to retain custody of her and having her walk out of our lives for fifty-one long weeks. She was only fourteen and fifteen at the time. Feelings of total depression, utter helplessness, frustration anger and bitterness followed. Now, three years later, I still

143

have all those feelings with, thank God, the exception of depression, which I slowly managed to overcome. All we ever wanted was to include our elder daughter's birth family into ours, instead we almost lost our daughter for good. Our younger daughter's open adoption is working well.

There is no doubt of Lois and Taff's intentions always to do the best for their daughters, and certainly it would seem that their way of managing contact has worked well for Catherine. Ultimately any discussion as to the reasons why contact did not work out as they wished for Selina is speculative. We should take account of the fact that their current perspective may well change, and it would be very helpful to interview them at a future point. It does seem possible that the manner in which they opened up contact, in combination with Selina's age, may offer some explanation for the way that it developed. Additionally, in terms of the evidence of the 1986 interview and the recent statement, the expectation that Selina's birth mother and her family were happy just "to be part of our extended family" may not perhaps have been carefully enough considered.

8 Matthew and Annabel

Lynne and Lyndsay adopted Matthew and Annabel in infancy. At the time of the follow-up interview Matthew was eighteen and Annabel thirteen. Lynne and Lyndsay also have a birth daughter, Emma, who was at that time sixteen. Their marriage ended some years before the interview in 1992, and they share the care of their three children. Annabel always had contact with her birth mother, Andrea. Attempts to establish contact for Matthew with his birth family proved unsuccessful until just a few months after he was originally interviewed in 1986.

Interviewer: *Matthew, in 1986 you said how much you wanted to know your birth mother, "but that" (this is something you said) "it would be pretty hard because I wouldn't know what to say". What was it in fact like when you first met Sue?*

Matthew: *It was very casual. Mum found out about her and we just went round to her house 'cause it's round in Heathcote which is just round the corner from where we live really. Basically we just went round for tea, I think. Then I got invited to go back again the next week and so I went back. It was a very casual meeting. We didn't have a lot in common because ... it was more like meeting another older lady, just an older lady that I knew. Not like a birth mother, you know. There wasn't a lot that I could say, we just had a good talk and she showed me round her house - it wasn't anything serious.*

Interviewer: *You didn't feel any sort of instant connection with her at all that you can remember?*

Matthew: *No, not at all*

Interviewer: *So has that changed since then. Do you feel a different sort of feeling for her now that you've got to know her more?*

Matthew: *No, not really. Now that I'm older, though, I can understand it a lot better, but it's still a real casual relationship, you know. We talk to each other I ring her every few weeks. I sometimes go round there for tea. It's pretty casual.*

Matthew's indication that he discovered no filial feelings towards his mother is in many ways consistent with his account in 1986 when he indicated that his search for his mother was less a search to discover her than it was to discover himself, through having a fuller picture and by making connections. The research findings, as noted earlier (see chapter four), seem generally to confirm this as a common response. In 1986, however, in addition to wanting to know about such things as where Sue lived and worked, Matthew said that it would be important to see "what she looked like, if she looked like me...". In this interview Matthew conveys the impression that it was hard to establish any immediate link with his mother. It would have been useful to have discussed how his feelings of connectedness might have been different had there been a regular exchange of information and photographs over the years, since in Matthew's case his adoptive parents had no substantial information. The high level of support which Matthew received from his adoptive parents, and his mother in particular, in arranging the meeting with his birth mother, Sue, were important to his first contact.

Matthew clearly approves of the fact that first contact was a low-key meeting without highly raised expectations. Once again the role played by his adoptive parents in helping it to be so was probably very important. Matthew also mentions that he is able to understand the idea of adoption more clearly because he is older. Conversely, in 1986, at age thirteen, he saw his age as potentially a major barrier to successful contact with his birth mother. In that interview he said this:

It would be pretty hard because I wouldn't know what to say. Because I would know more about her than I did before and it would be harder. Because when Annabel was little she didn't really understand.

He was then asked, "so you think that Annabel grew up with it, is that what you mean?", and he replied that this was so. Matthew's indication that his level of understanding increased, including through early adolescence, is consistent with the research of Brodzinsky and his colleagues (1984a, 1984b, 1992).

Interviewer: *Something else you said back in 1986 was that you had a feeling of sadness at not knowing her. This is what you said:*

Sometimes, when I'm in bed I just wish I could, I wish I knew her and what she looked like and everything else. I'd like her to want to see me but she might not want to see me because it might be too hard for her.

Interviewer: *Were you aware of any of those feelings when you met that it was difficult for her meeting you after all those years?*

Matthew: *I think it was difficult for her. But once the initial meeting was over it got a lot easier, once she'd met me, you know, going round there and she was coming round to see me sometimes and we went out occasionally, had breakfast - we still do that sometimes.*

Interviewer: *Did you find it did put away for you that feeling of sadness, that it's not there any longer, the feeling you talked about in 1986?*

Matthew: *Yes, it's gone. I'm more complete now, I know who she is, and I can go round to see her if I want to. I can do anything like that now. I don't have any questions or anything like that now. Or if I do I can ask her.*

Interviewer: *It's filled in the gaps for you?*

Matthew: *Yes*

Though Matthew stresses the informality of his relationship with Sue, it is important to note he indicates that his

147

relationship with her has been helpful to him in terms of creating a greater sense of wholeness since his information needs have now been met. It is also important to consider that Matthew recognises that he could continue to have questions he would want answered. This is clearly one of the significant advantages of a continuing relationship for adopted people with their original families.

No matter how thorough life work is with children and young people who are adopted, it is never possible to predict with accuracy what their information needs may be when they are older. When I asked Matthew about his understanding of the reason for his adoption back in 1986 he indicated that it related to the fact that his birth mother was too young to be able to parent him herself. There is little doubt that at age thirteen his answer would have been more complex had further information been available. His parents, however, knew very little about Sue or her circumstances at the time of his adoption. Contact now provides an opportunity to establish such matters as Sue's relationship with her parents at the time of his birth; whether she was in a steady relationship; whether her decision was greatly influenced by lack of support; or perhaps a wish to continue in education, or an inability to manage financially. Brodzinsky and his colleagues (1984a, 1984b) have emphasised how important age-appropriate explanations are for adopted and young people.

Interviewer: *Annabel you've always had contact with Andrea. You don't remember when you first had contact with Andrea because that was so early on, but how's your relationship developed since 1986?*

Annabel: *Pretty much the same really as Matthew, very casual. She comes round once a month, we ring each other, comes for special events, special things like school plays, and yes she's just like a family friend or maybe a sister I haven't seen for a while.*

Interviewer: *So when you say she comes once a month, it's not that you organise it once a month?*

Annabel: No, she just arrives.

Interviewer: *When I interviewed you in 1986, you were eight years old. I think you'd only recently turned eight. You described how the boys in your class were pretty slow to understand the meaning of adoption. You said this:*

Well they say to me that I'm adopted and they say that I'm stupid because they think I've got three or four mothers, but I've only got two. And they, er, some people that are in our class are adopted haven't met their birth mothers yet and they say that I'm real lucky because I've got them and I just say to the boys to be quiet about it.

Interviewer: *Do you find that adoption is something you talk about much these days with other people?*

Annabel: *Not really, it's just a part of my life. If it does come up it's really casual.*

It is interesting to note that both Matthew and Annabel describe a high level of reciprocity in their relationships with their birth mothers. It is also noticeable that both relationships in some ways have parallels with the sorts of informal relationships that adolescents often enjoy with their friends. It seems clear from the discussion with both that they play key roles in negotiating with their respective birth mothers the level of contact that they themselves want in their relationships. Neither, at this point at least, expresses any strong feelings that could be described as a parent/child relationship, though Annabel certainly describes a closer relationship than Matthew when she says that Andrea is like a 'family friend', or even perhaps a 'sister'. No doubt her contact over a much longer period contributes to her description of a closer relationship with Andrea than Matthew does with Sue. There may also be sex differences, however, in relation to the use of affective language, and greater ease in describing same sex-closeness and identification which could help to account for the difference.

The absence of parent/child descriptions in their relationships would seem to be attributable to the fact that they make a clear distinction between parenting and the biological status of being a parent. It is also worth noting that neither Matthew nor Annabel was particularly keen to be involved in these further interviews, since both described adoption as a very ordinary fact of life and found it hard to understand why anyone would wish to re-interview them!

Annabel's comment in 1986 concerning the fact that the boys in her class think she's perhaps got three or four mothers, even though she states she has only two, is interesting. Again, this emphasises the need for the adoption story to be a continuing one, and it highlights the necessity to build into parenting by adoption ways for children and young people to update their adoption stories. Children of eight may not understand completely the nature and meaning of adoption (Brodzinsky *et al*, 1984a, 1984b). Certainly the boys in Annabel's class also demonstrate appreciable gaps in their understanding of human biology! Annabel did not make a clear distinction in 1986 between the respective roles of her two mothers, as she does now in 1992.

Interviewer: *One of the biggest fears of adoptive parents, especially for teenage children, is if they have contact that there could be a time when they lose their children, that they might run off to their birth families. Do you think that's a realistic fear?*

Annabel: *I think if they're told about them when they're young and it's not made up to be a big event in a big way. If it's normal and casual then I don't think it is. If it's really casual.*

Interviewer: *So by casual you mean treated as a normal part of life?*

Annabel: *Yes.*

Interviewer: *But otherwise you think there could be a risk that that could happen?*

Annabel: It depends what type of person you are. I mean, I wouldn't go running off. Mum's mum and dad's dad. I think everyone has fights and arguments, it's part of life, so I personally wouldn't but it depends what type of person you are.

Matthew: *I wouldn't run off, because, like Annabel said, I've got my mother and father and, as well, I don't see Sue as my mum so I wouldn't run off to live with her. I don't think of her as a mother really, she's just another friend.*

The question about adolescents running away to their birth families is an important one in the light of the previous interview. Annabel's answer seems a sensible one. Fights and arguments are normal for adolescents running away is not particularly unusual either. What Annabel seems to be saying is that if you have learned to live with an ongoing relationship with your original family which, to use her words "is casual", then things are not likely to get out of proportion so that you want to run away to them.

In Annabel's case as was noted her birth mother Andrea met Lynne and Lyndsay at the time of placement. There then followed a period of direct contact between them by post and then telephone leading to face to face contact again when Annabel was five years old. From that time contact has been regular but not organised in any formal way, and Annabel herself may now take a lead role in initiating it. It is important to note again the clear distinction that both Matthew and Annabel make between the role of being a parent and the status of being a [birth] parent.

Interviewer: *When you look at your own birth families, do you see things in yourself, talents you have or interests that you've had or things about yourself that you can trace back to them?*

Matthew: *No, not really. She's got the same colour hair as me but that's about all. We don't have a lot in common. I've been brought up differently to how she lives. She lives in a nice cottage over in Heathcote and her husband races pigeons and I'm not really interested in pigeon racing so ...*

Interviewer: *What about personality characteristics?*

Matthew: *No, there's not a lot really, no. We are both a lot different. I think it's just the way I've been brought up.*

It is interesting that when Matthew is asked about the similarities he finds in respect of his mother he seems to consider the question in terms of observable physical characteristics and activities. Matthew would argue for the influence of environment over heredity, and it is not surprising to see how a young man whose current consuming passion is surfing could wonder how much he might have in common with his birth mother, whose partner is similarly passionate about pigeon racing! It is also true that it requires a sophisticated level of analysis to identify personality characteristics and traits. Were Matthew to be interviewed again in several years it would be interesting to see whether he recognised other similarities with his birth mother.

Interviewer: *The contact that both of you have had has mostly been with birth mothers and their families. What about contact with your birth fathers?*

Matthew: *I haven't had any contact at all with my birth father.*

Annabel: *We've tried to make contact with him but he's married now and he wants to leave it and I think I feel the same. I didn't have any choice in finding my mother, and maybe if had I just found out recently I would want to find out about both parents, but I think just knowing Andrea is enough.*

It is the common experience of agencies offering post-adoption services that adopted people who are seeking contact with original families are most likely to be seeking, at least initially, a reunion with their birth mothers (see for example McMillan and Hamilton, 1993). In part the explanation for this is obvious. Whatever the circumstances of their birth and their early childhood, all adopted people know that they had a nine-month 'in utero' relationship with their mothers. They may not always be certain about the nature of the relationship they had with their birth fathers, and birth fathers may also be much more difficult to trace as their names may not be on the birth records.

Adopted people who trace their mothers may often go on to trace other members of their family, however. In some instances this may happen very quickly as a natural consequence of contacting their mothers. In other instances it may involve a separate search which once again will be highly demanding in terms of emotional energy. Annabel seems to suggest that for the meantime at least she feels she has sufficient contact with her family of origin through her relationship with Andrea. In part this seems related to the length of time she has known Andrea, and she indicates she may not want a new relationship to set alongside it. It is possible that this derives from a sense of loyalty to Andrea and it may also of course change. She has, in addition, however, learned that her birth father does not seem particularly interested in meeting her, so her answer in part may be a protection against that rejection. In Matthew's case the impression was gained that at some future point he may wish to have contact with his father. As Lynne indicates in the next interview, his father's whereabouts are known should Matthew wish to contact him.

Interviewer: *So are there any things that either of you would want to say to other young people your ages about adoption or about contact?*

Annabel: *Basically that it's just a casual thing. It's just like having a friend of the family who's not the same as mum. If you take it really seriously it could have some problems, but not if you are just casual about it and maybe if you get told when you are younger. I think it's so much easier to be brought up with knowing than it would be to break it to you when you were fifteen.*

Interviewer: *So you mean not only being told at a young age, but having contact at a young age, or do you just mean being told?*

Annabel: *Contact, I think, because I'm not really sure, but it would be a lot easier than when you're older. You think about it more and you're more worried about it than when you're younger.*

Where adoption with some form of contact is considered in this country it is often only where children already have established links with their original families. The experience of young adopted people, like Annabel, who have had contact in some form from the outset and who now manage it in a very easy and accepting way, should prompt us to reconsider this conventional practice wisdom.

9   Lynne and Andrea

Lynne, Annabel's adoptive mother, has known and had contact with Andrea, Annabel's birth mother, since the time of the adoption.

Interviewer: *Lynne and Andrea, I've just been talking with Matthew and Annabel about their adoption and Annabel was talking about the contact she's had with you, Andrea, over the years since she was adopted. I wonder what memories the two of you have of the first contact that you had with each other.*

Lynne: *I remember it being an extremely emotional meeting, probably because I wasn't really sure of how it was going to be. I'd always imagined it was going to be a meeting in an office situation and as it turned out it was at the hospital with Annabel there.*

Andrea: *I think it was almost like shell-shock - it didn't really hit me until a long time after. The deep meaning of how much it had meant, came to me later, much later, probably even years later. But at the time I think it was all pretty fast and very emotional and lots of feelings flying about.*

Interviewer: *So you've had a lot of contact on and off over the last thirteen years. How would you describe your relationship now?*

Lynne: *Good friends, but it's actually more than that, somehow. I always feel that Andrea is part of the family. We've got an ever-enlarging family and Andrea is part of it. So it's like I think we've established a really good friendship. We share somebody very special. But it is more than that.*

Andrea: *In a lot of ways I think I'm closer to Lynne probably than my own sisters through the Annabel link.*

Interviewer: *So do you feel that Lynne is part of your family as well?*

Andrea: *Oh I do, yes I do.*

The opportunity for Lynne and Lyndsay (Annabel's father) to meet Andrea at the time of the placement doubtless had a major effect on the way that contact subsequently developed. As already indicated (see chapter four), it is not uncommon for adoptive parents to attribute a feeling of reassurance to the contact they have. Where this has existed from the outset, it can be seen as particularly significant in helping them to feel better about parenting somebody else's child. Interviews with members of original families, where there have been such meetings, often lead to descriptions of a feeling of comfort in being able to picture the family that their child will be with (Dominick, 1988; Fratter, 1989; Field, 1990; McRoy, 1991; Rockel and Ryburn, 1988).

It is important to note that Annabel's and her family's relationship with Andrea is not static. It has gone through many changes and has been transformed over the years to the point where there is currently an appreciable bond of closeness. Though this may often not exist, and is not necessary for contact to be successful, it undoubtedly contributes to the sense of partnership there is in Andrea's relationship with her daughter and her adoptive family.

One way to ensure that there is a greater likelihood that original families and adoptive families can form links is to create systems in which original families are active participants in the selection of the new family. This is common practice in countries where there is more open practice, and was suggested as a possible change in the initial Adoption Law Review discussion documents (DOH, *Paper 1*, 1990, p. 60, para. 100). In circumstances where there have been contested proceedings which have been determined in favour of the local authority, the involvement of original families in having some say in the new family for their child can begin to address the feelings of powerlessness they seem commonly to describe (see Ryburn,

1994, in preparation). Joan Fratter's research (1991) indicates that even in circumstances where adoptions are thought likely to be contested, original families can be engaged at the level of discussing plans for future contact with their children or young people.

Lynne's acknowledgement that she and Andrea 'share somebody very special' can serve as a reminder of the fact that whether there is a *continuing* relationship in terms of contact or not, there is, nonetheless, always a *relationship* between adoptive families and original families.

There is a noticeably greater sense of reciprocity in Andrea's relationship with Annabel and her adoptive family than was described by Lois and Taff in their interview in 1986, and this also emerges clearly in the final interview (see chapter ten).

Lynne: *I think what's been good though is that we've both been able to respond when the need has been there, if I had really wanted to see Andrea or Annabel to see her. Something came up last year and Annabel was the lead in the school production, and it felt really important that Andrea should come along to that too. So that was a time when there was something specific for us to share, and we made that contact again then and sat side by side, two mums ...*

Andrea: *Watching our daughter on stage (laughter)!*

One of the features of successful contact is its flexibility, and the way that it alters over time with changing circumstances. An ultimate aim of contact is to permit children and young people who are adopted the ability to negotiate the level of contact that seems right for them. There can be an agreement at the outset of placement which acknowledges that contact will be important, and the parties can make a commitment to maintain it in some form for all their sakes. This sort of agreement has been used with great success in open adoptions in the United States (Etter, 1993). To seek to prescribe the forms future contact should take would be unrealistic, and it is important to see written agreements as working documents that are under constant review.

Interviewer: *Andrea, I remember talking to you many years ago now and you said this: "I can liken adoption to a cut or a wound. Having contact, you see that you're cut and you're bleeding and you do get pain, but because of the contact you can keep on using the limb or the hand so that you will regain the use of it". That was the way you described adoption for you and that was 1985 in fact. Is that how you still see it?*

Andrea: *I do. I think just to add the years on to that, the cut or the wound has healed and the limb is still working.*

Two principal reasons are often advanced for severing all contact at adoption. First, that it makes it more likely children and young people will attach successfully to their new families. This cannot be sustained by the research findings, (see chapter four).

The second is that it is easier for members of original families to come to terms with the loss of their child or young person. The extract from the 1986 interview with Lorette (see above chapter five) highlights the impossibility of grieving a living loss in the absence of a continuing relationship. Andrea's image of adoption as a wound for birth parents that contact slowly heals is a graphic one, which the research supports (Dominick, 1988; Fratter, 1989; Field, 1990).

Interviewer: *Andrea, you were saying there were no regrets on your part as you look back. I wonder if in your wider family there are regrets or whether the sort of relationship you've built up with Annabel has healed their cuts as well.*

Andrea: *My mother still has not and will never come to terms with it. I suppose in her generation it was just absolutely unheard of and that really saddens me for Annabel's sake, because I think at times she must feel really cut out or that she's done something wrong or that she's not recognised as part of that family, and that saddens me terribly.*

Lynne: *But that also can happen in normal families. I think it's very easy to say that's because we're talking about an adoptive situation here. I do think that can happen in any family where maybe Grandma doesn't accept somebody or relationships get a bit confused. I think it's really important to see it for what it is. OK there may be times where there may be some guilt involved, I guess, especially for grandparents and some fears. I guess your mother was concerned about you not getting hurt.*

Adoption practice has often not recognised its ripple effects on birth parents' extended family networks. The adversarial nature of court proceedings can all too easily, even in the early stages of a family's involvement with statutory services, create a climate in which there is a rapidly narrowing range of options, so that adequate consideration is not given to the role wider family networks can play in the lives of their children and young people. Jane Rowe and her colleague's research (1984), for example, showed that where grandparents were involved in the lives of young people in long-term care, this was almost wholly beneficial. The study, involving some 400 children in the care of six different authorities, also revealed that in only one of the authorities was there any significant contact between grandparents and their children in care. The breadth of vision necessary, therefore, to see the crucial role for wider family involvement depended on agency policy, attitudes and values. More often than not, the research also indicates, key decisions about contact are not made in any planned or conscious way but by default through planning inertia (Millham *et al*, 1986; Vernon and Fruin, 1986). There is also every indication (see for example Trent, 1989) that wider family has not always received sufficient consideration as a placement resource.

Andrea's comment is a useful reminder, not only of the wide-reaching effects that adoption decisions will have, but of the fact that there will probably seldom be a unanimity of view in any wider family about what is best for its children and young people. Lynne's observation, on the other hand, that divisions are present in any family, highlights the importance of not seeing issues and conflicts in terms of pathology, where adoption is involved.

Interviewer: *The children don't have any substantial contact with their fathers at all and I was wondering about that?*

Lynne: *Yes, it's something that concerns me as the issue has come up at various times. I guess the short answer to a very long and involved situation is that it's basically up to the children, I think. If they want to pursue contact and it's right for them, then it's right. I think the issue of their birth fathers' contact is a slightly different one, in that there has been no contact at all.*

Andrea: *That's right, on my side there's been none.*

Lynne: *And Matthew's is much the same, there's been nothing. I do know where both the birth fathers are and the children both know that, but as yet they've not expressed a wish to pursue that. If they did and they thought it was right for them, then that would happen.*

Interviewer: *So your guide is very much what Matthew and Annabel are asking for?*

Lynne: *Yes, definitely.*

Andrea: *And I think our guide all the way along has been that.*

Lynne: *Yes.*

The issue of contact with birth mothers has been discussed already in relation to the interviews with Chris and Joanne and Matthew and Annabel (see chapters six and eight). Chris, in particular, highlighted how the issues of control over important decisions can assume special significance for adopted people. It is important to note Lynne's view, therefore, that should contact occur, it is essential the children themselves take the initiative in pursuing it. There is a clear contrast here with the approach which Lois and Taff chose in relation to their daughters.

Interviewer: *I was going to go on to ask you a little bit more about that because in addition, Lynne, to being a parent by adoption you also have a role as a post adoption-counsellor. I wondered what your professional experience as well as your personal experience have taught you about making contact with people - whether there's a right age, whether there's a right way to do it?*

Lynne: *I think as far as there being a right age, I really do believe the earlier contact is established the better, because everybody is growing up knowing everybody else. Children are incredibly accepting when they are young and it's a lot easier. I think my own situation has shown that, with Matthew meeting Sue when he was so much older.*

Lynne, as Matthew himself did earlier, contrasts the potential difficulty for older children in establishing contact when it has not existed from the outset, compared with the experience of someone like Annabel who always grew up with it. As has been noted in chapter four, Lynne's comment that children can accept a great range of different sorts of relationships if they grow up with them, finds support in research, such as Schaffer and Emerson's (1964). It would nonetheless be unusual in open adoption for members of original families to play a substantive role in the care and upbringing of their birth children, though this can always be a possibility. We should note on the other hand, that depth of attachment is not necessarily a correlate of the amount of time spent together in a relationship (see for example Fox, 1979; Rutter, 1980).

Interviewer: *Do you think it's important that adoptive parents be able to get on with birth families in order for contact to work?*

Lynne: *I think it's the ideal, but it may not happen. It's as I said, families are made up of so many different characters and personalities, and in non-adoptive families those same dynamics are there. I think there is also a time when the adoptive parents have to take a back seat and I think that's happened now, especially with Matthew being that much older. I let Sue and Matthew establish their own pace and they work out between the two of them what they want to do. But Sue and I also have a relationship between us too which in a way is quite a separate thing. And that feels really good, because it feels like Matthew and Sue have set up their own relationship and I think that's going to happen as Annabel gets older. Yes, I sort of feel like you [speaking to Andrea] and I will be able to maintain the friendship that we've got, but your relationship with Annabel will become something far more between the two of you.*

It would be unrealistic to expect adoptive families and original families to be able, necessarily, to relate effectively to each other. Where the original family has participated in the selection of the new family for their child there is probably more likelihood of effective relationships from the outset, and of continuing contact. This seems to be the case even following contested adoptions (Ryburn, 1994, in preparation).

Relationships in open adoption require time and commitment, like any relationship, in order to grow and develop. There will be periods in relationships in open adoption when there is more or less closeness, perhaps periods when all parties do not get on well or where there may even be open conflict. Openness, however, provides a framework within which negotiation can occur to accommodate changing needs and circumstances. Lynne highlights here the importance of Matthew's being able to set his own pace in his relationship with Sue. Where relationships are established for older children, it may be a long time before any satisfactory equilibrium is found. Joanne, by her own account, took more than two years to feel that her new relationship with her original family was grounded in reality.

Interviewer: *I guess a key word that both Matthew and Annabel used about their relationships with their birth families, was that the relationship should be 'casual',. The fact that it was casual was important.*

Lynne: *Yes, very much so. I think for them because it's been so comfortable and so casual it's almost a non-issue. You know, it's not something that comes up over and over at home at all. We seem to have established a really comfortable working family relationship, don't we?*

It is useful to broaden discussion at this point to consider contact in general for children and young people who are not being parented by their original families. The work of the Dartington researchers (Millham *et al*, 1986, 1990) as well as that of others (Fisher *et al*, 1986) shows how difficult it can be to sustain successful contact with original families. Contact can also very often be established in ways that make it unlikely to be successful.

In 1986 the Dartington study highlighted how issues such as the lack of a clear role during contact meetings for members of original families, the setting in which contact takes place, its frequency, the degree of encouragement and support given to maintain it, can all be crucial to its success. High levels of expectation are seldom helpful since anything that falls short of the ideal is likely to be seen as a failure. In Matthew and Annabel's case the fact that their relationships with their original families have been able to develop in a very low-key and informal way has doubtless been an important ingredient in their success.

Interviewer: *Lynne, I was wondering from your experience working in post-adoption whether you believe there is a minimum level of contact that all children in adoption should have regardless of whether the adults are able to get on very well together.*

Lynne: *I think it's really important that that option is there. Not just at the beginning when the placement takes place, when there's a lot of information available. Children throughout their earlier years have times when there are things that they need to know, they need the answers. To be able to say, "Well let's find out," yes it's a great and affirming thing. "There is something out there I need to know and we can find out." I think you had an example of that ...*

Andrea: *Yes, even up until recently Annabel and I and the family were sitting about and Annabel and I were comparing knees and ankles and wrists and fingers, even now 13 years down the track.*

Interviewer: *So just something as basic as where do your physical characteristics come from?*

Andrea: *Yes. "I wondered if you'd get my knobbly knees or whatever", that sort of stuff.*

It is helpful to contrast Lynne's approach to meeting her children's identity needs with the approach adopted by Lois and Taff who decided that it was important that they gather information themselves and form a relationship prior to opening things up for their children. It is useful also to reflect that it is never possible at a point that a new permanent placement is arranged to predict with accuracy what the information needs of any child or young person will be as they grow.

The only interview which could not be followed up from 1986 was an interview with Sue and Richard. In their interview in 1986, which describes their experiences of meeting thirty-four years after Richard's adoption, Richard recounts that the most significant thing for him, on meeting his mother, was to learn that she had developed a passion for collecting and restoring old things. This was something that had also absorbed him throughout childhood and adulthood. He indicated that as a child this hobby had set him aside from other children. When this fact was placed in the context of his being adopted it had contributed to his feeling very different from other children. Discovering he shared this interest with his mother, Sue, was for him part of what he described in 1986 as, "joining the human race".

It would be highly unlikely that any social worker, however skilled, who was involved in placing Richard, could have recognised the great significance that such an outwardly minor piece of information about his mother might assume.

Though it is possible to make some predictions about the information that many adopted people may want to acquire through contact with original families, in each case, needs vary enormously. Some of the obvious information that adopted people will be likely to want concerning their original family relates to physical characteristics. Photographs and written information, however, as Chris has said (see chapter six), give only a "glimpse of a life". The level of information sought can at times be conveyed only in direct contact. Annabel's wish to consider, in a detailed way, the parallels between her physical characteristics and those of her mother are a good example. In 1986 Chris, talking about the contact that she has with Lorraine, her birth mother, described the great significance for them both of similarities they discovered in body language and things such as their handwriting. In the same series of interviews Sue and Richard (see above introduction to part two) described the importance of discovering a similar idiosyncratic speech pattern.

The ready availability, through contact, of a source of direct information about things that children and young people need to know concerning their original families can be very important. Where adoptive parents are consistently unable to meet the growing information needs of their children there is some possibility that the trust between parent and child, the key ingredient for effective parenting, is diminished. Continuing contact certainly provides the most effective means of ensuring that accounts given to children and young people continue to be relevant and to meet their needs.

Interviewer: *A lot of adopted parents are concerned about contact. They feel that they might lose their children ultimately through contact and occasionally adopted children may go to live with their birth families. I wondered whether you were concerned with Matthew at perhaps a vulnerable age, thirteen - entering adolescence, having contact?*

Lynne: *I don't know if threatened is the word. I felt some concern, not that I was going to lose him but that it might change our relationship in some way. And it has, it's changed it for the better. But the thing I've learned is that love is an infinite thing. Because somebody else now gets another bit it doesn't mean you're getting less. It means there's plenty for everybody. Maybe that's some of the fear that adoptive parents have, that because there may be a birth mother, now part of the family if*

165

you like, the child won't love them as much, that they are actually going to lose something.

Andrea: *They think of it as a piece of pie and there's only so much to go round, and they don't realise that love's not like a pie, it's not four bits or two bits.*

Lynne: *Pies can be pretty big (laughter). The other thing I think that I've discovered, and that I believe, is that if you love your children - I'm speaking as an adoptive parent here - if you love your children, you too want to truly know who they are. To me it seems if you can acknowledge that your children have birth parents and another family out there, another set of grandparents - you know people with blue eyes when your family are all brown eyed - if you can acknowledge that, it's like you're acknowledging the very essence of the children themselves. And I think what that does is take away a lot of the fear. I always had the feeling that even if my children had to go away from me to be more part of this contact, that they would come back. It's like we're all part of it together.*

Lynne's commitment to continuing contact, as being best for her children, is obvious. It is important to note that she was also recruited by an agency with a similar commitment. Unless those recruiting prospective adopters believe in the advantages of various forms of continuing contact then it is unlikely that prospective adopters will want actively to embrace the idea. As Fratter concluded (1989), it is possible to recruit adopters who wish to continue contact with original families. A key determinant in her view, is whether the agency itself is committed to contact.

Lynne identifies the principal reason for the fear that prospective adopters can feel as the idea that the maintenance of contact will weaken attachments in children's new families. This idea finds it paralleled in the theoretical ideas of Goldstein and colleagues (1973, 1979). Lynne's and Andrea's conclusion, on the other hand, almost echoes the words of Schaffer, summarising research on multiple attachments:

Certainly the fear that that [the parental] relationship is going to be 'diluted' by the simultaneous existence of other relationships is quite unjustified: a child's attachment is not some limited quantity that has to be divided up amongst people.

(1990, p. 83)

Lynne's final comment is in many ways a clear restatement of David Kirk's original thesis (1964, 1981). As she indicates, the capacity for adoptive parents to respect, identify and acknowledge the different qualities which their children have, qualities which are not derivative of their lives in their adoptive families, is at the heart of an ability to recognise "the very essence of the children themselves". Sarah, (see chapter ten) in the final interview, describes how for her acknowledgement of difference has been a significant benefit in her adoptive parenting. Such acknowledgement is also recognising the inextricable link that adoption establishes between different families.

Interviewer: *Most of our talk and most openness in adoptions centres on women or birth mothers having relationships often with adoptive mothers. I wondered about the men out there. Where are they?*

Lynne: *In my work I certainly deal with a lot more birth mothers than birth fathers, but the birth fathers I do see have no less depths of pain and anguish over what has happened than the birth mothers. I would equally encourage the birth fathers to make the contact if that is something they wish to happen. I also have some real concerns for those children who are now being born as a result of the new birth technologies, IVF, the artificial insemination by donor and the gift programmes, because the information on their backgrounds is not so freely available. The pain and anguish I see out there in the adoption arena can be laid at the feet of secrecy. The openness and the ability to get the information that people need, be it a birth parent, an adoptee, and even an adoptive parent , seems such a basic right.*

Lynne's final linking of the information needs in adoption with those of children born as a result of donor-assisted conception programmes, is an important one. The recent Human Fertilisation and Embryology Act (1990) does provide in section 13(5) that "a woman shall not be provided with treatment services unless account has been taken of the welfare of any child who may be born as a result of the treatment (including the need of that child for a father), and of any other child who may be affected by the birth." It also provides in section 31 that children may, after 18 years (or in some cases earlier), receive counselling in their own right concerning the provision of information relating to their genetic origins. There is, however, no provision for the disclosure of identifying information, except for certain purposes connected with proceedings in England and Wales under the Congenital Disabilities (Civil Liability) Act 1976. Thus, access to significant and useful information will often be denied those born as a result of donor fertility treatments. For some of those people there could be the sense of loss and difficulty in identity achievement that has sometimes confronted adopted people.

10 Sarah, Neil, Robin, Charlotte, Maria, Marc and Gina

Sarah and Neil adopted Robin in 1984, and at the time of the follow-up interview he was seven-and-a-half years old. Almost from the outset there was substantial contact with Maria and Tom, his birth parents, and their wider families. Shortly after they were interviewed in 1986 Maria and Tom ended their relationship, though each continued independent contact with Robin. Tom's contact was substantial prior to his departure for Canada in mid-1991.

Maria has been in a relationship with Marc since 1988 and they have an eighteen-month-old daughter Gina. Marc agreed to participate in the interview also. Robin, though present, was too shy of the camera to participate!

Neil and Sarah subsequently adopted Charlotte in October 1986, and at the time of this interview she was five-and-a-half years old. Her birth family was always clear that they did not seek the extensive contact that there has been with Robin, though there has been some contact with her birth mother, Bridget, and both her grandmother and her great grandmother.

Interviewer: *Neil and Sarah, what's it been like having two very different adoptions in the family?*

Sarah: *Well, I suppose the first thing to say is that we wanted two the same but, I think it was obvious right from the start when we first met Bridget that it wasn't going to be possible, and I think it was a gradual process of getting used to the idea that it was going to be different. The most obvious difference is that we don't know anything really about Charlotte's birth father and probably never will, so it did mean that if there was any contact it was going to be through Bridget and her family.*

Neil: *Yes, I think we've come to accept that they are different and they are like your own relatives, you just have different relationships with different ones. It's just the way it is.*

Sarah: *I think when people start to ask questions like, "What's it going to be like later on when they grow up?", I mean of course we don't know that, but when you enter into any relationship you don't know what the outcome is going to be. You just work through that relationship.*

It is not uncommon for adoptive parents to express concern about the different levels of information or contact that they have in relation to children adopted from different original families. Lois and Taff sought to address this situation by ensuring that they established a similar level of contact and information for each of their daughters. When asked in the 1986 interview what they would have done had they been able to establish contact for one daughter but not for the other, they indicated that they would probably not have proceeded with contact at all.

The alternative view of Neil and Sarah is that parenting requires an individual approach, since all children have different and differing needs. A prescribed level of contact for one child in the family would doubtless not be the right level of contact for another child. They would argue that effective parenting does not depend on an ability to treat each child the same. Neil indicates that having contact at some level for both of their children has 'normalised' their relationships. They now put the differences in their relationships with their children's original families on a par with the differences that we ordinarily expect in relationships with different family members and different branches of our extended family networks. As Sarah goes on to say, there is always the potential for difficulty in any relationship. It is a matter of trying to establish it at the outset on a basis that means that re-negotiation for changing circumstances is possible, whilst accepting there will always be a measure of unpredictability.

Interviewer: *Maria, in 1986 when I asked you if you were very aware of the fact that you were Robin's birth mother, you had this to say:*

Well I don't know, I guess I do know that I am his birth mother and all that, but I don't think about it in a parent sort of way because I'm on the outside, I'm just a friend you know. There's no maternal connection with him at all. It's like seeing a cousin. It's not like he's mine or anything like that.

Interviewer: *I wonder whether having Gina has changed your feelings about that?*

Maria: *No, I still feel that way. As he's got older there's little things that he's done and I'd think "Oh my God that's just like Tom" or I'd see a lot of Tom in him. I don't know whether you see so much of yourself. I mean I don't go looking for me in him but he has his little mannerisms, I suppose so there is still something there. But I don't have the emotional feelings I feel about Gina, the 'maternal things' that come gushing out and you get choked up about. I don't know whether I've suppressed it with Robin or not but I don't feel they are there because I didn't do any of the right things to trigger them off in the first place. I mean, I just look at the way he's growing up and his relationship with Sarah and Neil and he's so happy with them and I still think I made the right decision. I mean I made the decision with Tom I don't know how he feels about it, but I certainly feel really good about it still.*

Interviewer: *I'm sorry that Tom is in Canada and can't be with us today, but does any of you have any idea how he might respond if I were to put that question to him?*

Maria: *I think Sarah's best to answer that.*

Sarah: *I think Tom is quite emotional about Robin. I mean going to Canada was tied around not leaving before Robin's birthday, and I think that was significant in terms of how Tom feels about Robin. I think Tom recognises how like him Robin is and he probably is more intensely emotional about him. I don't think*

Tom regrets Robin being adopted, but I do think that it's an experience he doesn't wish to repeat.

This section of the interview raises an important consideration: to what extent will members of original families feel connected to, for example, their sons, daughters, grandchild, brother or sister, through the maintenance of contact. Maria's comment that she continues to have no great sense of maternal connection to Robin finds a parallel in the comments of Matthew and Annabel who describe their relationships with their birth mothers other than in terms of son or daughter relationships. Sarah indicates on the other hand, that she imagines Tom has feelings of a rather stronger connection to Robin.

There is also the issue as to how safe it ever feels for original family members to express those feelings, if they exist. Maria acknowledges this to some extent when she says it's something that she may have suppressed in relation to Robin. She also says, however, that the development of close attachments occurs through the medium of a close relationship of the sort she has never had with Robin. This is consistent with the research on attachment (Rutter, 1979). It is interesting however, to reflect on the fact that Neil, Robin's adoptive father, in the interview in 1986, stated:

I think one of the things that has happened is ... I've found as it's gone along that I now think of Maria and Tom being Robin's birth parents more than I did at the beginning ... and I feel really good about that. I previously sort of did think about them as in an aunt and uncle role, and I think as I get into it I do think of us as the adoptive parents and them as the birth parents and it just sort of feels very comfortable.

Interviewer: *Marc, had you had any experience of adoption before you met Maria?*

Marc: *I have a close friend who I went to school with and he was adopted. That's really the only sort of contact I've had with adoption.*

172

Interviewer: *So was it difficult for you to enter a relationship with Maria and then also enter into a relationship with Robin and Robin's adoptive family?*

Marc: *Personally, no. The whole set-up of the adoption seems to be so natural that it doesn't seems to be a problem.*

Interviewer: *Is there anything that surprised you at the outset when you first talked about it with Maria?*

Marc: *Well, we never really talked about it that much. I think the first time we just went around to Sarah and Neil's place. That's when the reality hit me I suppose, but as I said it was so natural that it just seems to be that's how it is.*

Marc's observations here are worth noting. He states that the ordinariness of the relationships between Maria and Robin's adoptive family meant that something which to outsiders would perhaps be unusual to him seemed very "natural". Thus he was able to take it at face value as being "how it is".

Interviewer: *Neil, in 1986 you had this to say:*

It seems to be such a natural thing, the four of us and Robin. If it's not confusing for us I don't think it will be confusing for him. I think it's just going to be a fact of life, it's just the way it's going to be and I think he'll grow up accepting it just as we do.

Interviewer: *Do you still feel that?*

Neil: *Yes, I think that hasn't changed. It just seems even more so now really. I think though we probably felt more intense about it then, and as time goes on because it seems so natural, it just becomes more and more a fact of life and just the way things are.*

Interviewer: *Do you agree Sarah?*

Sarah: *Yes, I don't sort of try and rationalise what we do any more, we just do it and I think I expect that for Robin it is just part of his life.*

The issues raised here follow on from the discussion with Marc. There have now been over seven years of open and very informal contact between Robin and his original family. The degree of intensity that was present in 1986 no longer exists, because as Neil says, contact has become "more and more a fact of life ... just the way things are".

Interviewer: *So Sarah, back in 1986, talking about Maria and Tom coming round, you said:*

I think initially when they used to come round I was anxious that they might judge me as a parent and I think I do try hard for all of us, but I think I also try hard because I am aware of the fact that he is adopted, and it was a long time in coming and so I do feel that I have to try hard anyway as a parent.

Interviewer: *Do you still feel that you try extra hard as an adoptive parent?*

Sarah: *Yes, in some situations, yes I do. I think that probably the time when I might now is if something goes wrong and Maria's there. I now think I'm parenting a different ... you know, I'm parenting Robin, and Robin's Robin. And I think whatever Maria might think of me as a mother she's never going to have to experience what I'm going through because Gina's not Robin. You know, that it doesn't matter what Robin's like at seven. She won't go through that with Gina. Yes, I suppose I'm more relaxed about it now.*

Interviewer: *So has that continuing contact over the years helped change your feelings, or is it something else that makes you feel different?*

Sarah: *No, I think I've just come to accept it. I think that in terms of before I might have decided that I had to try and explain things to Maria. Now I just think Maria has to work it out for herself. Like there was a lovely classic example when Maria and Marc moved into their house and we went round there. Robin walked in there and said something to the effect of ...*

Maria: *He said it was a "junk yard".*

Sarah: *Yes, "junk yard" or a "dump" because there were boxes everywhere, and Maria was mortally offended.*

Maria: *Well it was a reaction, wasn't it, from both of us, and it was natural.*

Sarah: *But I just decided in the end, well you know I can't be responsible for everything Robin says and feels.*

Maria: *No, I don't expect you to be, I mean that was fine!*

Adoptive parents often describe feelings of added responsibility in parenting a child not born to them. Whether they are likely to be more or less aware of this responsibility when they have continuing contact with their child's original family is difficult to say. With or without such contact adoptive parents face constant reminders that they parent a child who has a different birth heritage. The feeling of responsibility that Sarah expressed in the interview in 1986 has diminished over the years, though she herself would not attribute that particularly to the continuing contact that there has been. She does, on the other hand, relate it to the passage of time. If there had not been continuing contact, time would in a sense have been 'frozen time', with no continuing relationship to offer a context within which a diminishing sense of responsibility could have occurred. Sarah describes herself as now being at a point where she does not feel, as an adoptive parent, that she has to be especially responsible for her son's behaviour or views and she is able to permit Maria to make what sense she wishes of these.

Interviewer: *So are there any other things that you would say are different for you now compared with 1986, for any of the three of you?*

175

Sarah: *Well I think initially when you go into open adoption you are looking for answers to some of the questions you might have about the background or whatever, and as time goes by well those answers are had. So you are not looking for things like that. And like, I don't think, "Oh Robin hasn't seen Maria lately, we just go round there". It's more a question of "We haven't seen Maria and Marc and Gina lately, it's time we went round there". It's really not got a lot to do with Robin's exposure to his birth mother, it's more to do with us as two separate families.*

Maria: *Yes.*

Neil: *And early on you are more concerned probably with the issues of adoption, but later on, when that becomes more or less an established thing, there are so many other issues come along. Schooling and other things that you worry about for developing children means that your concerns move on to other things.*

One of the interesting things about the relationship that Neil and Sarah have developed with Maria and Marc and Maria's wider family, as well as with Tom and his wider family, is the high degree of reciprocity in their relationships. This is very much a move away from the old idea of access in which there is managed contact, with an obligation on original family members to fit with an arrangement that has been organised for them. The most common parallel is good foster care placements. Here foster carers recognise the importance and value for children, wherever it is possible, of easy informal contact. This is at best neither stressful nor demanding and may take place either at the foster carers, or the original family's home. In this way, as Neil describes it in their situation, the important issues in the relationship become the ordinary day-to-day issues, rather than the issues that centre on Robin's status as an adopted child.

Sarah: *I think one real worry was when it became pretty obvious there were going to be glaring differences between Robin's adoption and Charlotte's adoption. I worried about that for quite a while in terms of how I'd explain it. But the reality is that Charlotte is a very different child from Robin and you actually can say to Charlotte, "You won't know anything about your birth father", and know that Charlotte will accept that. And that, "your birth mother's in England" and "no she won't be coming to see you", and Charlotte I think accepts it more. You just have to give her credit for coping with a different relationship, instead of feeling guilty because you didn't put her into the same relationship. You just have to give her some credit for coping with the differences.*

Maria: *And there's things that she does like latching on to Tom and Marc as her special people as well.*

Interviewer: *Does having the amount of contact that you do with Maria and also with Tom sometimes stand in the way of being able to parent Robin effectively?*

Neil: *No, I'm sure it's a help because when you're parenting and you don't understand say, Robin's behaviour, it's a great thing to have an inside input. Because you know Maria and because you know Tom, that insight's good.*

Sarah: *It's also meant we've been able to avoid some of the pitfalls. Tom spoke frequently about having a fairly unhappy time at primary school and some of the difficulties he had, and I think we've, I suppose, in a way modified Robin's behaviour, I hope, so that we will avoid ...*

Neil: *Modified our own behaviour.*

Sarah: *Yes, well both really ...*

Neil: *Yes.*

Sarah: *Modified ours so that Robin doesn't fall into the same traps that Tom did.*

Neil: *But having said that we don't have that sort of insight with Charlotte do we?*

Sarah: *No.*

Neil: *Not to anything like the same extent. But it doesn't seem such an issue with Charlotte does it? It didn't seem that we needed it as much as with Robin.*

Sarah: *No. We know of some things, like we've talked when we have met with the birth grandmother and the great grandmother of Charlotte, which is usually at her birthday. My sister's (Anne) usually there and Anne's said things like, "Charlotte's a natural nurse, you know she knows how to treat people who are unwell and what to say to them," and the grandmother said, "oh my sister's a nurse, you know", so you get that sort of information. And Charlotte's very athletic and good at gym and Lyndsay's (Charlotte's grandmother) able to say, "well so was Bridget". And I've said things to Bridget like "Charlotte goes to bed late, gets up late and keeps her room in a tip", and she's said, "yes that's what I'm like." So I mean it's those sorts of things ...*

Neil: *It's the little things that you learn that become very important though. You know you find real significance in those.*

Sarah's comment that there are inevitably differences between any two children in respect of the relationships that can exist with their original families is commonsense, yet nonetheless worth re-stating. As was the case for Matthew and Annabel, until Matthew established contact with his birth mother at the age of thirteen, there are quite different levels of contact for Robin compared with Charlotte. Though there are times when this could doubtless pose some difficulties, in neither of these instances has there been insurmountable problems. The children themselves seem to have been readily able to accept the differences and accommodate them.

Neil and Sarah's discussion about the value to them in parenting Robin, of the detailed knowledge that they have about his birth parents is one of the greatest benefits that adoptive parents describe in relation to open adoption (Ryburn, 1991). With Charlotte they demonstrate how even the much more limited knowledge and information they glean through their ongoing relationship with her family is useful as a source of reassurance in parenting her. The sorts of links they describe being able to make would probably not be possible in any relationship unless there was at least some direct contact.

Sarah: *I think, too, I'm a lot more relaxed about Charlotte as her own person and that there's nothing of me or my temperament in Charlotte. In many ways I enjoy Charlotte because she's totally different. I feel very proud, you know. People must wonder who don't know she's adopted, because I'll stand back and say, "**my** child is very good at gym, she's very athletic", and I can say that. I think they might wonder at me, but I admire that in her. I admire her lean trim figure and her ability to tackle anything new with no fear. I'm not like that. I get a lot of pleasure out of that difference really.*

Sarah's acknowledgement of difference here is entirely consistent with David Kirk's thesis (1964, 1981) concerning effective adoptive parenting. It is interesting to hear her describe the great satisfaction she gains as a parent from that difference. It seems very likely that continuing contact has heightened this awareness and ultimately helped her to regard it so positively.

Interviewer: *The responses of some people watching the video in 1986 was that "This is too good to be true", or "This can't last", or, "it's unreal." It's now six years on, what would the three of you say to people that said that?*

Neil: *If I have to reflect back to '86, I think then that I thought we were pretty special, and pretty lucky in having an open adoption which seemed to be working really well, and I don't feel that any more. I now more or less think, "Well that's just the way it is, isn't it?"*

Maria and Sarah: *Yes.*

Conclusion

Perhaps the single most important observation to emerge from this book is that openness is likely to contribute to a sense of normality in adoption relationships. This normality or ordinariness, is accomplished by a willingness to recognise and confront issues as they arise, the welcome acceptance of difference, a willingness to negotiate new arrangements to meet each relationship's changing circumstances, and a wish to avoid taking decisions that have irrevocable consequences. These approaches locate adoption relationships within the range of relationships with which we all live. They help reduce the 'special significance' which may militate against the achievement of realistic hopes, goals and expectations.

Secrecy in adoption has sometimes created a climate of fear and hostility in the divide between the two lives of adopted children. It has served as an encouragement to ignore difference and has neglected the importance for children of their birth inheritance. It is more likely for these reasons to lead to an upbringing which fails to offer to adopted children two of the three elements that Triseliotis identified from his studies (1983) as necessary for healthy identity formation. These two elements, full and complete knowledge about the past, and a belief in others' perceptions of oneself as a worthwhile person, are likely to work in tandem. Where, therefore, growing knowledge of a different birth inheritance is not apparently valued for its own sake, this may lead adoptees to the conclusion that if their families of origin are not valued perhaps, by implication, neither are they.

David Kirk's widely supported thesis (1964) that the key to successful parenting in adoption lies in the acknowledgement of difference is not, paradoxically, incompatible with the achievement of ordinariness. This is because it is uniqueness, rather than the merging of difference, that is arguably what most of us can accept as ordinary and normal. This is borne out by our capacity to accommodate a dramatic transformation in the forms of family life, when only a few decades ago the "two parents two birth children" family was the norm. Openness and open practice allow for what Goffman, (1961, p. 127) once called "unique outcomes". Secrecy, on the other hand, is the failure to celebrate difference, born of the fear that to do so will breach the relationship between adopters and their children.

Openness and open practice are both cause and consequence of the acknowledgement of difference. As Lynne remarked in chapter nine:

If you love your children, I'm speaking as an adoptive parent here, you too want to truly know who they are. To me, it seems if you can acknowledge that your children have birth parents and another family out there, another set of grandparents - you know people with blue eyes when your family are all brown eyed - if you can acknowledge that, it's like you're acknowledging the very essence of the children themselves. And I think what that does is take away a lot of the fear. I always had the feeling that even if my children had to go away from me to be more part of this contact, that they would come back. It's like we're all part of it together.

I would like to leave the last lines of this book for an adopted person.

> **I am a ghost written book**
> **My author's names**
> **are nowhere on my spine**
> **But inside, look - -**
> **the pair**
> **haunt every line**

Elizabeth Morgan
London, 1983

References

Chapter one: The law, the judiciary and openness

DHSS, (1983), *Code of Practice: Access to Children in Care*, London: HMSO.

DHSS, (1985), *Review of Child Care Law: Report to Ministers of an Inter-Departmental Working Party*, London: HMSO, September 1985.

DoH, (1990), *Inter-Departmental Review Of Adoption Law: 1: The Nature and Effect of Adoption*, London: HMSO.

Fratter, J., (1991), "Parties in the Triangle", *Adoption and Fostering*, 15:4, 91-8.

Fratter, J., (1989), *Family Placement and Access: Achieving Permanency for Children in Contact with Birth Parents*, Ilford: Barnardos.

Griffith, K., (1991), "Access to Adoption Records: The Results of Changes in New Zealand Law", in Mullender, A., [ed.], *Open Adoption: The Policy and the Practice*, London: BAAF.

Griffith, K., (1981), *Adoption: Procedure, Documentation, Statistics, New Zealand 1881 - 1981*, Wellington: Published by the author.

Hodgkins, P., (1987), *Adopted Adults: An Evaluation of their Relationships With Their Families,* Oxford: NORCAP.

Houghton Report, (1970), *Adoption of Children: Working Paper*, London: HMSO.

Houghton Report, (1972), *Report of the Departmental Committee on the Adoption of Children*, London: HMSO, Cmnd. 5107.

Howe, D., (1990), "The Consumers' View of the Post Adoption Centre", *Adoption and Fostering*, 14:2, 32-37.

Howell, D., and Ryburn, M., (1987), "New Zealand: New Ways to Choose Adopters", *Adoption and Fostering*, 11:4, 38-40.

Lowe, N., Murch, M., Borkowski, M., Copner, R., Griew, K., (1991), *Report of the Research into the Use and Practice of Freeing for Adoption Provisions,* Bristol: Socio-Legal Centre for Family Studies, University of Bristol.

Millham, S., Bullock, R., Hosie, K., Little, M., (1989), *Access Disputes in Child-Care,* Aldershot: Gower.

Mullender, A., (1991), "The Spread of Openness in New Zealand - the Ends of the Process Meeting in the Middle", in Mullender, A., [ed.], *Open Adoption: The Philosophy and the Practice*, London: BAAF.

Short Report, (1984), *Second Report From the House of Commons Social Services Committee, "Children in Care",* London: HMSO.

Rowe, J., (1989), "Chance of a Lifetime", *Adoption and Fostering*, 13:3, 1-2.

Ryburn, M., (1991a), "The Myth of Assessment", *Adoption and Fostering* 15:1, 20-27.

Ryburn, M., (1991b), "Making the Children Act Work: Professional Attitudes and Professional Power", *Early Child Development and Care*, 75, 71-78.

Ryburn, M., (1992), "Family Group Conferences", in Thoburn, J., [ed.], *Participation in Practice: Involving Families in Child Protection*, Norwich: University of East Anglia.

Stevenson, P., (1991), "A Model of Self Assessment for Prospective Adopters", *Adoption and Fostering*, 15:3, 30-33.
Trent, J., (1989), *Homeward Bound*, Ilford: Barnardos.

Triseliotis, J., (1991), "Identity and Genealogy in Adopted People", in Hibbs, E., *Adoption: International Perspectives*, Madison CT: International Universities Press.

van Keppel, M., (1991), "Birth Parents and Negotiated Adoption Agreements", *Adoption and Fostering*, 15:4, 81-90.

Chapter two: Identity formation

Adams, G., Shea, J., (1979), "The relationship., Between Identity Status, Locus of Control, and Ego Development", *Journal of Youth and Adolescence*, 8, 81-89.

Anderson, H., and Goolishian, H., (1987), "Problem Determined Systems: Towards Transformation in Family Therapy", *Journal of Strategic and Systemic Therapies*, 5:4, 1-13.

Baran, A., Sorosky, A., Pannor, R., (1975), "Secret Adoption Records: The Dilemma of Our Adoptees", *Psychology Today*, 9:7, 38-42.

Bateson, G., (1980), *Mind and Nature: A Necessary Unity*, New York: Bantam Books.

Berger, P., and Luckmann, T., (1967), *The Social Construction of Reality*, Harmonsworth: Penguin.

Baumeister, R., (1986), *Identity: Cultural Change and the Struggle for Self*, New York: Oxford University Press.

Brodzinsky, D., Schechter, D., Braff, A., and Singer, L., (1984), "Psychological and Academic Adjustment in Adopted Children", *Journal of Consulting and Clinical Psychology*, 52:4, 582-590.

Brodzinsky, D., Radice, C., Huffman, L., and Merkler, K., (1987), "Prevalence of Clinically Significant Symptomatology in a Nonclinical Sample of Adopted and Non Adopted Children", *Journal of Clinical Child Psychology*, 16, 350-356.

Derrida, J., (1974), *Of Grammatology,* Baltimore: John Hopkins University Press.

Derrida, J., (1978), *Writing and Difference,* Chicago: University of Chicago Press.

Derrida, J., (1984), *Dissemination,* Chicago: University of Chicago Press.

Deutsch, D., Swanson, J., Bruell, J., Cantwell, D., Weinberg, F., and Baren, M., (1982), "Overrepresentation of Adoptees in Children With the Attention Deficit Disorder", *Behavior Genetics,* 12, 231-238.

Erikson, E., (1956), "The Problem of Ego Identity", *Journal of the American Psychoanalytic Association,* 4, 56-121.

Erikson, E., (1959), "Identity and the Life Cycle", *Psychological Issues,* 1, comprises whole monograph.

Erikson, E., (1968), *Identity: Youth and Crisis,* New York: Norton.,

Erikson, E., (1980), *Identity and the Life Cycle,* New York: Norton.

Gilligan, C., (1982), *In a Different Voice,* Cambridge MA: Harvard University Press.

Hoopes, J., (1982), *Prediction in Child Development: A Longitudinal Study of Adoptive and Non-Adoptive Families,* New York: Child Welfare League of America.

Howard, S., and Kubis, J., (1964), "Ego Identity and Some Aspects of Personal Functioning", *Journal of Psychology,* 58, 459-466.

Howe, D., and Hinings, D., (1987), "Adopted Children Referred to a Child and Family Centre", *Adoption and Fostering,* 11:3, 44-47.,

Hult R., "The Relationship, Between Ego Identity Status and Moral Reasoning in University Women", (1979), *Journal of Psychology,* 103, 203-207.

Humphrey, M., and Ounsted, C., (1963), "Adoptive Families Referred for Psychiatric Advice", *British Journal of Psychiatry*, 109, 599-608.

Kohlberg, L., (1964), "Development of Moral Character and Moral Ideology", in Hoffman, M., and Hoffman, L., [eds.], *Review of Child Development Research*, vol., I, New York: Sage.

Marcia, J., (1966), "Development and Validation of Ego Identity Status", *Journal of Personality and Social Psychology*, 3, 551-558.

Marcia, J., (1967), "Ego Identity Status: Relationship, to Change in Self-Esteem, "General Maladjustment", and Authoritarianism", *Journal of Personality*, 35, 119-133.

Marcia, J., (1980), "Identity in Adolescence", in Adelson, J., [ed.], *Handbook of Adolescent Psychology*, New York: Wiley.

Marcia, J., and Friedman, M., (1970), "Ego Identity Status in College Women" *Journal of Personality*, 38, 249-63.

Maturana, H., and Varela, F., (1987), *The Tree of Knowledge: The Biological Roots of Human Understanding*, London: New Science Library.

Mead, G., (1934), *Mind, Self and Society*, Chicago: University of Chicago Press.

Norvell, M., and Guy, R., (1977), "A Comparison of Self-concept in Adopted and Non Adopted Adolescents", *Adolescence*, 12, 443-448.

Offer, D., (1973), *The Offer Self Image Questionnaire*, Chicago: Psychiatry Department, Michael Reese Media Centre.

Offer, D., Aponte, J., and Cross, L., (1969), "Presenting Symptomatology of Adopted Children", *Archives of General Psychiatry*, 20, 110-16.

Plomin, R., and DeFries, J., (1985), *Origins of Individual Differences in Infancy: The Colorado Adoption Project*, Orlando FL: Academic Press.

Read, D., Adams, G., and Dobson, W., (1984), "Ego-Identity, Personality and Social Influence Style", *Journal of Personality and Social Psychology*, 46, 169-77.

Richardson, L., (1913), "The Measurement of 'Mental' Nature and the Study of Adopted Children", *Eugenics Review*, 4, 391-4.

Rockel, J., Ryburn, M., (1988), *Adoption Today: Change and Choice in New Zealand*, Auckland: Heinemann/Reed.

Rothman, K., (1984), "Multivariate Analysis of the Relationship, of Personal Concerns to Adolescent Ego Identity Status", *Adolescence*, 19, 713-727.

Rowe, I., and Marcia, J., (1980), "Ego Identity Status, Formal Operations, and Moral Development", *Journal of Youth and Adolescence*, 9, 87-99.

Ryburn, M., (1994), "Post Adoption Contact Following Contested Adoption Proceedings", in preparation.

Sachdev, P., (1991), "The Triangle of Fears: Fallacies and Facts", in Hibbs, E., [ed.], *Adoption: International Perspectives*, Maddison CT: International Universities Press.

Schechter, M., Carlson, P., Simmons, J., and Work, H., (1964), "Emotional Problems in the Adoptee", *Archives of General Psychiatry*, 10, 37-46.

Schenkel, S., and Marcia, J., (1972), "Attitudes Toward Premarital Intercourse in Determining Ego Identity Status in College Women", *Journal of Personality*, 3, 472-482.

Schoenberg, C., (1974), "On Adoption and Identity", *Child Welfare*, 53, 549.

Seglow, J., Pringle, M., and Wedge, P., (1972), *Growing Up Adopted*, Windsor: National Foundation For Educational Research in England and Wales.

Stark, P., and Traxler, F., (1974), "Empirical Validation of Erikson's Theory of Identity Crises in Late Adolescence", *Journal of Psychology*, 86, 25-33.

Stein, L., and Hoopes, J., (1985), *Identity Formation in the Adopted Adolescent*, New York: Child Welfare League of America.

Tan, A., Kendis, R., Fine, J., and Porac, J., (1977), " A Short Measure of Eriksonian Ego Identity, *Journal of Personality Assessment*, 41, 279-84.

Toussieng, P., (1962), "Thoughts Regarding the Etiology of Psychological Difficulties in Adopted Children", *Child Welfare*, 41, 59-65.

Triseliotis, J., (1973), *In Search of Origins*, London: Routledge and Kegan Paul.

Triseliotis, J., and Russell, J., (1984), *Hard to Place*, Aldershot: Gower.

Waterman, A., (1982), "Identity Development From Adolescence to Adulthood: an Extension of Theory and a Review of Research", *Developmental Psychology*, 18, 341-58.

Waterman, A., (1990), "Personal Expressiveness: Philosophical and Psychological Foundations", *Journal of Mind and Behavior*, 11, 47-74.

Chapter three: Identity in adoption
Aboud, F., (1987), "The Development of Ethnic Self Identification and Attitudes", in Phinney, J., and Rotheram, M., [eds.], *Children's Ethnic Socialisation: Pluralism and Development*, Newbury Park CA: Sage.

Amin, K., and Oppenheim, C., (1992), *Poverty in Black and White: Deprivation and Ethnic Minorities*, London: CPAG.

Andujo, E., (1988), "Ethnic Identity of Transethnically Adopted Hispanic Adolescents", *Social Work*, 33, 531-35.

Bagley, C., (1993), "Transracial Adoption in Britain: A Follow-up Study, With Policy Considerations", *Child Welfare*, 72, 285-299.

Barn, R., (1990), "Black Children In Local Authority Care: Admissions Patterns", *New Community*, Commission For Racial Equality, 16:2, 229-246.

Barn, R., (1993), "Black and White Child Care Careers, A Different Reality", in Marsh, P., and Triseliotis, J., [eds.], *Prevention and Reunification in Child Care*, London: Batsford/BAAF.

Barnardos, (1988), *Maintaining Contact: Partnership in Practice: Networks Video*, London: Barnardos.

Bebbington, J., and Miles, A., (1989), "The Background of Children Who Enter Local Authority Care", *British Journal of Social Work*, 19:5, 349-368.

Becker, S., and MacPherson, S., [eds.], (1989), *Public Issues Private Pain*, London: Insight/Carematters.

Becker, S., and Silburn, R., (1990), *The New Poor Clients: Social Work, Poverty and the Social Fund*, Wallington Surrey: Community Care/Benefits Research Unit.

Bertocci, D., and Schechter, M., (1991), "Adopted Adults' Perception of Their Need to Search: Implications for Clinical Practice", *Smith Studies in Social Work*, 61:2, 179-96.

Bhatt, A., [ed.], (1988), *Britain's Black Population: A New Perspective*, The Radical Race Statistics Group, Aldershot: Gower.

Bradshaw, J., (1990), *Child Poverty and Deprivation in the UK*, London: National Children's Bureau.

Brodzinsky, D., Schechter, D., Braff, A., and Singer, L., (1984a), "Psychological and Academic Adjustment in Adopted Children", *Journal of Consulting and Clinical Psychology*, 52, 4, 582-90.

Brodzinsky, D., Singer, L., and Braff, A., (1984b), "Children's Understanding of Adoption" *Child Development*, 55, 869-78.

Brodzinsky, D., Schechter, M., and Henig, R., (1992), *Being Adopted: The Lifelong Search for Self*, New York: Doubleday.

Brown, G., and Harris, T., (1978), *Social Origins of Depression: A Study of Psychiatric Disorder in Women*, London: Tavistock.

Charles, M., Rashid, S., and Thoburn, J., (1992), "Research on Permanent Family Placement of Black Children and Those From Minority Ethnic Groups", *Adoption and Fostering*, 16:2, 3-4

Chestang, L., (1972), "The Dilemma of Bi-Racial Adoption", *Social Work*, 17, 100-05.

Chimuzie, A., (1975), "Transracial Adoption of Black Children", *Social Work*, 20, 296-301.

Coleman, J., and Hendry, L., (1980), *The Nature of Adolescence*, London: Routledge and Kegan Paul.

Coleman, J., (1974), *Relationships in Adolescence,* London: Routledge and Kegan Paul.

Commission for racial Equality, (1992), *Annual Report 1991*, London: CRE.
Davey, A., (1983), *Learning to be Prejudiced: Growing up, in Multi Ethnic-Britain*, London: Edward Arnold.

DoH, (1990), *Letter to Directors of Social Services*, 20th January.

DoH, (1991), *The Children Act Guidance and Regulations, Volume 3, Family Placements*, London: HMSO.

DoH/Welsh Office, (1992), *Review of Adoption Law: Report to Ministers of an Interdepartmental Working Group*, London: DoH/Welsh Office.

Erikson, E., (1959), *Identity and the Life Cycle: Selected Papers by Erik H., Erikson: vol., 1, Psychological Issues*, New York: International Universities Press.

Feigelman, W., and Silverman, A., (1983), *Chosen Children*, New York: Praeger.

Feldman, S., and Elliott, G., [eds.], (1990), *At The Threshold: The Developing Adolescent*, Cambridge MA: Harvard University Press.

Festinger, L., (1957), *A Theory of Cognitive Dissonance*, Stanford CA: Stanford University Press.

Fratter, J., (1988), "Black Children with Black Families", in Argent H., [ed.], *Keeping the Doors Open: A Review of Post Adoption Services*, London: BAAF.

Fratter, J., (1989), *Family Placement and Access: Achieving Permanency for Children in Contact With Birth Parents*, Ilford: Barnardos, 1989.

Fratter, J., Rowe, J., Sapsford, D., and Thoburn, J., (1991), *Permanent Family Placement: A Decade of Experience*, London: BAAF.

Frisk, M., (1964), "Identity problems and Confused Conceptions of the Genetic Ego in Adopted Children During Adolescence", *Acta Paedo Psychiatrica*, 31, 6-12.

Gill, O., and Jackson, B., (1983), *Adoption and Race: Black, Asian and Mixed Race Children in White Families,* London: Batsford/BAAF.

Goffman, E., (1963), *Stigma: Notes on the Management of Spoiled Identity*, Harmondsworth: Penguin.

Gorer, G., (1965), *Death, Grief and Mourning*, London: Cresset Press.

Government Statistical Service, (1993), *Social Trends*, vol. 23, London: HMSO.

Griffith, K., (1981), *Adoption: Procedure, Documentation, Statistics, New Zealand 1881-1991*, Wellington: Published by the author.

Grow, L., and Shapiro, D., (1974), *Black Children-White Parents*, New York: Child Welfare League of America.

Harrison, A., (1985), "The Black Family's Socialising Environment: Self-Esteem and Ethnic Attitude among Black Children", in McAdoo, J., and McAdoo, L., [eds.], *Black Children*, Newbury Park CA: Sage.

Hinton, J., (1976), *Dying*, Harmondsworth: Penguin.

Hogg, A., Abrams, D., and Patel, Y., (1987), "Ethnic Identity, Self Esteem and Occupational Aspirations of Indian and Anglo Saxon British Adolescents", *Genetic, Social and General Psychology Monographs*, 113, 487-508.

Howe, D., and Hinings, D., (1987), "Adopted Children Referred to a Child and Family Centre", *Adoption and Fostering*, 11:3, 44-47.,

Howe, D., Sawbridge, P., and Hinings, D., (1992), *Half a Million Women: Mothers Who Lose Their Children by Adoption,* London: Penguin.

Jaffee, B., and Fanshel, D., (1970), *How They Fared in Adoption*, New York: Child Welfare League of America.

Jaynes, G., and Williams, R., (1989), *A Common Destiny: Blacks and American Society*, Washington DC: National Academy Press.

Johnson, P., Shireman, J., and Watson, K., (1987), "Transracial Adoption and the Development of Black Identity at Age Eight", *Child Welfare,* 66, 45-55.

Kaye, K., and Warren, S., (1988), "Discourse About Adoption in Adoptive Families", *Journal of Family Psychology*, 4, 406-33.

Klein, M., (1932), *The Psycho-Analysis of Children*, London: Hogarth Press.

Kirk, D., (1964), *Shared Fate: A Theory of Adoption and Mental Health*, New York: Free Press.

Kirk, D., (1981), *Adoptive Kinship; A Modern Institution in Need of Reform,* Toronto: Butterworths.

Kornitzer, M., (1971), "The Adopted Adolescent and the Sense of Identity", *Child Adoption*, 66, 43-8.

Kowal, K., and Schilling, K., (1985), "Adoption Through the Eyes of Adult Adoptees", *American Journal of Orthopsychiatry*, 55, 345-62.

Kubler-Ross, E., (1975), *Death: The Final Stage of Growth*, Englewood Cliffs NJ: Prentice-Hall, Inc.

Ladner, J., (1977), *Mixed Families*, New York: Anchor/Doubleday.

Lambert, J., (1970), *Crime Police and Race Relations*, Oxford: Oxford University Press.

Lifton, B., (1979), *Lost and Found: The Adoption Experience*, New York: Dial Press.

Marris, P., (1974), *Loss and Change*, London: Routledge and Kegan Paul.

McEwan, E., [ed.], (1990), *Age the Unrecognised Discrimination*, London: Age Concern.

McRoy, R., Grotevant, H., and Zurcher, L., (1988), *Emotional Disturbance in Adopted Adolescents: Origins and Development*, New York: Praeger.

McRoy, R., Zurcher, L., Lauderdale, M., and Anderson, R., (1982), *Self Esteem and Racial Identity in Transracial and In-racial Adoptees*, Springfield Ill: Charles C., Thomas.

McRoy, R., Zurcher, L., (1983), *Transracial Adoptees: The Adolescent Years*, Springfield Ill: Charles C., Thomas.

McRoy, R., Zurcher, L., Lauderdale, M., and Anderson, R., (1984), "The Identity of Transracial Adoptees", *Social Casework*, 65, 34-39.

McWhinnie, A., (1967), *Adopted Children: How They Grow Up*, London: Routledge and Kegan Paul.

Morrall, M., and Ryburn, M., (1986), *Adoption in the 1980's*, [video and teaching notes], Christchurch NZ: Shipley's Vision and Sound.

Morris, J., (1991), *Pride against Prejudice: Transforming Attitudes to Disabilities*, London: Women's Press.

National Association of Citizens Advice Bureaux, (1991), *Barriers to Benefits: Black Claimants and Social Security*, London: NACAB.

Ogbu, J., (1987), "Opportunity Structure, Cultural Boundaries and Literacy", in Langer, J., [ed.], *Language, Literacy and Culture: Issues of Society and Schooling*, Norwood NJ: Ablex.

Parkes, C., (1972), *Bereavement: Studies of Grief in Adult Life*, New York: International Universities Press.

Peters, M., (1985), "Racial Socialization of Young Black Children", in McAdoo, J., and McAdoo, L., [eds.], *Black Children*, Newbury Park CA: Sage.

Phinney, J., Lochner, B., and Murphy, R., (1990), "Ethnic Identity Development and Psychological Adjustment in Adolescence", in Stiffman, A., and Davis, L., [eds.], *Ethnic Issues in Adolescent Mental Health*, Newbury Park CA: Sage.

Piaget, J., (1963), *The Origins of Intelligence in Children*, New York: Norton.

Piaget, J., (1964), *Judgment and Reasoning in the Child*, Paterson NJ: Littlefield, Adams.

Picton, C., and Bieske-Vos, M., (1982), *Persons in Question: Adoptees in Search of Origins*, Melbourne: Published by the author.

Pinker, R., (1993), "A Lethal Kind of Looniness", *Times Higher Education Supplement*, 10th September.

Raynor, L., (1980), *The Adopted Child Comes of Age*, London: Allen and Unwin.

Rickarby, G., and Egan, P., (1980), "Issues of Preventive Work With Adopted Adolescents", *Medical Journal of Australia*, 1, 470-72.

Rockel, J., and Ryburn, M., (1988), *Adoption Today: Change and Choice in New Zealand,* Auckland: Heinemann/Reed.

Rotheram, M., and Phinney, J., (1987), "Definitions and Perspectives in the Study of Children's Ethnic Socialization", in Phinney, J., and Rotheram, M., [eds.], *Children's Ethnic Socialization: Pluralism and Development*, Newbury Park CA: Sage.

Rowe, J., and Lambert, L., (1973), *Children Who Wait*, London: ABAA.

Rowe, J., Hundleby, M., and Garnett, L., (1989), *Child Care Now: A Survey of Placement Patterns*, London: BAAF.

Ryburn, M., (1991), "Openness and Adoptive Parents", in Mullender, A., [ed.], *Open Adoption: The Philosophy and the Practice*, London: BAAF.

Ryburn, M., (1992a), "Advertising for Permanent Placements", *Adoption and Fostering,* 16:2, 8-15.

Ryburn, M., (1992b), "Contested Adoption Proceedings", *Adoption and Fostering*, 16:4, 28-38.

Ryburn, M., (1994, in preparation), "Birth Parents and Contested Adoption", in Ryburn, M., [ed.], *Contested Adoption Proceedings*, Aldershot: Gower/Arena.

Ryburn, M., (1994, in preparation), "Adoptive Parents and Contested Adoption", in Ryburn, M., [ed.], *Contested Adoption Proceedings*, Aldershot: Gower/Arena.

Sachdev, P., (1991), "The Triangle of Fears: Fallacies and Facts", in Hibbs, E., [ed.], *Adoption: International Perspectives*, Maddison CT: International Universities Press.

Sants, H., (1964), "Genealogical Bewilderment in Children with Substitute Parents", *British Journal of Medical Psychology*, 37, 133-41.

Seligman, M., (1975), *Helplessness*, San Francisco: Freeman.

Shireman, J., and Johnson, P., (1986), "A Longitudinal Study of Black Adoptions: Single Parents, Transracial and Traditional", *Social Work* 31, 172-76.

Simon R., and Alstein, H., (1977), *Transracial Adoption*, New York: Wiley.

Simon R., and Alstein, H., (1981), *Transracial Adoption: A Follow-up*, Lexington MA: Lexington Books.

Simon R., and Alstein, H., (1987), *Transracial Adoptees and Their Families: A Study of Identity and Commitment*, New York: Praeger.

Simon R., and Alstein, H., (1992), *Adoption, Race, and Identity: From Infancy Through Adolescence*, New York: Praeger.

Small, J., (1986), "Transracial Placements: Conflicts and Contradictions", in Ahmed, S., Cheetham, J., and Small, J., [eds.], *Social Work With Black Children and Their Families*, London: Batsford/BAAF.

Sorosky, A., and Pannor, R., (1978), T*he Adoption Triangle*, New York: Doubleday/Anchor.

Spencer, M., (1983), "Children's Cultural Views and Child Rearing Strategies", *Developmental Review*, 4, 351-370.

Spencer, M., and Dornbusch, S., (1990), "Minority Youth in America", in Feldman, S., and Elliott, G., [eds.], *At the Threshold: The Developing Adolescent*, Cambridge MA: Harvard University Press.

Stiffman, A., and Davis, L., [eds.], (1990), *Ethnic Issues in Adolescent Mental Health*, Newbury Park CA: Sage.

Stone, F., (1969), "Adoption and Identity", *Child Adoption*, 58, 3, 17-28.

Thoburn, J., (1994, in preparation), "The Uses and Abuses of Research in Contested Adoptions", in Ryburn, M., [ed.], *Contested Adoption Proceedings*, Aldershot: Gower/Arena.

Thoburn, J., Rashid, S., and Charles, M., (1992), "The Placement of Black Children with Permanent new Families", *Adoption and Fostering*, 16:3, 13-18.

Torkington, P., (1991), *Black Health: A Political Issue*, Liverpool: Catholic Association for Racial Justice and Liverpool Institute of Higher Education.

Triseliotis, J., (1973), *In Search of Origins*, London: Routledge and Kegan Paul.

Triseliotis, J., (1983), "Identity and Security in Long Term Fostering and Adoption", *Adoption and Fostering*, 7:1, 22-31.

Triseliotis, J., (1991), "Identity and Genealogy in Adopted People", in Hibbs, E., [ed.], *Adoption: International Perspectives*, Madison CT: International Universities Press.

Chapter four: Research in open adoption

Barth, R., (1987), "Adolescent Mothers' Beliefs About Open Adoption", *Social Casework,* 68:6, 323-331.,

Belbas, N., (1987), "Staying in Touch: Empathy in Open Adoptions", *Smith College Studies in Social Work*, 57, 184-198.

Benet, M., (1976), *The Character of Adoption*, London: Jonathan Cape.

Barth, R., and Berry, M., (1988), *Adoption Disruption: Rates, Risks and Responses*, Hawthorne NY: Aldine de Gruyter.

Berridge, D., and Cleaver, H., (1978), *Foster Home Breakdown*, Oxford: Blackwell.

Bertocci, D., and Schechter, M., (1991), "Adopted Adults' Perception of Their Need to Search: Implications for Clinical Practice", *Smith Studies in Social Work*, 61, 179-96.

Borgman, R., (1982), "The Consequences of Open and Closed Adoptions for Older Children", *Child Welfare*, 61, 4, 217-230.

Borland, M., (1991), "Permanency Planning in Lothian Region", *Adoption and Fostering*, 15:4, 35-40.

Bouchier, P., Lambert, L., and Triseliotis, J., (1991), *Parting With a Child For Adoption: The Mother's Perspective,* London: BAAF.
Bowlby, J., (1952), *Maternal Care and Mental Health*, Geneva: World Health Organisation.

Brodzinsky, D., Schechter, D., Braff, A., and Singer, L, (1984a), "Psychological and Academic Adjustment in Adopted Children", *Journal of Consulting and Clinical Psychology*, 52 4, 582-90.

Brodzinsky, D., Singer, L., and Braff, A (1984b), "Children's Understanding of Adoption", *Child Development*, 55, 869-878.

Brodzinsky, D., Schechter, M., and Henig, R., (1992), *Being Adopted: The Lifelong Search for Self*, New York: Doubleday.

Bullard, E., Mallos, E., with Parker, R., (1990), *Custodianship Research Project: A Report to the Department of Health*, Bristol: Socio-Legal Centre for Family Studies, University of Bristol.

Burgoyne, J., and Clarke, D., (1984), *Making A Go of It*, London: Routledge and Kegan Paul.

Burgoyne, J., Ormrod, R., and Richard, M., (1987), *Divorce Matters,* Harmondsworth: Penguin.

Byrd, A., (1988), "The Case for Confidential Adoption", *Public Welfare*, 47, 3, 20-23.

DoH, (1991), *Patterns and Outcomes in Child Placement: Messages from Current Research and Their Implications*, London: HMSO.

DoH, (1991), *Interdepartmental Review of Adoption Law, - The Nature and Effect of Adoption,* Paper 1, London: DoH.

Dews, E., Hales, V., and Milner, I., (1993), *Planning for Permanence? An Inspection of Adoption Services in Three Northern Counties*, Leeds: Social Services Inspectorate/DoH.

Deykin, E., Campbell, L., and Patti, P., 'The Post Adoption Experience of Surrendering Parents', *American Journal of Orthopsychiatry,* 47:4, 271-280.

Dominick, C., (1988), *Early Contact in Adoption: Contact Between Birth Mothers and Adoptive Parents at the Time of and After Adoption*, Research Series No 10, Wellington: Department of Social Welfare.

Dunn, J., (1983), "Sibling Relationships in Early Childhood", *Child Development*, 54, 787-811.

Dunn, J., (1988), *The Beginnings of Social Understanding*, Cambridge MA: Harvard University Press.

Dunn, J., (1993), *Young Children's Close Relationships: Beyond Attachment*, London: Sage.

Dunn, J., and Kendrick, C., (1982), *Siblings: Love, Envy and Understanding*, Cambridge MA: Harvard University Press.

Etter, J., (1993), "Levels of Cooperation and Satisfaction in 56 Open Adoptions", *Child Welfare*, 72, 257-267.

Fanshel, D., and Shinn, E., (1978), *Children in Foster Care*, Columbia: Columbia University Press.

Field, J., (1991), "Views of New Zealand Birth Mothers on Search and Reunion", in Mullender, A., [ed.], *Open Adoption: The Philosophy and the Practice*, London: BAAF.

Fisher, F., (1973), *The Search for Anna Fisher*, New York: Arthur Fields.

Fisher, M., Marsh, P., Phillips, D., with Sainsbury, E., (1986), *In and Out of Care: The Experience of Children, Parents and Social Workers*, London: Batsford/BAAF.

Foster, A., (1973), "Who Has the Right to Know?", *Public Welfare*, 37 3, 34-37.

Fox, N., (1977), "Attachment of Kibbutz Infants to Mothers and Metaplet", *Child Development*, 48, 1228-39.

Fratter, J., (1991), "Parties in the Triangle", *Adoption and Fostering*, 15:4, 91-98.

Fratter, J., (1989), *Family Placement and Access: Achieving Permanency for Children in Contact with Birth Parents*, Ilford: Barnardos.

Fratter, J., Rowe, J., Sapsford, D., and Thoburn, J., (1991), *Permanent Family Placement: A Decade of Experience*, London: BAAF.

Fratter, J., (1992), Personal communication, September.

Goldstein, J., Freud, A., and Solnit, A., (1973), *Beyond the Best Interests of the Child*, New York: Free Press.

Goldstein, J., Freud, A., and Solnit, A., (1979), *Before the Best Interests of the Child*, New York: Free Press.

Gross, H., (1993), "Open Adoption: A Research-Based Literature Review and New Data", *Child Welfare*, 72, 269-284.

Hetherington, E., (1979), "Divorce: A Child's Perspective", *American Psychologist*, 34, 851-858.

Hetherington, E., (1988), "Parents, Children and Siblings: Six Years after Divorce", in Hinde, R., and Stevenson-Hinde, J., [eds.], *Relationships Within Families; Mutual Influences*, Oxford: Clarendon Press.

Hetherington, E., Cox, M., and Cox, R., (1985), "Play and Social Interaction in Children Following Divorce", *Journal of Social Issues*, 35, 26-49.

Hetherington, E., Cox, M., and Cox, R., (1985), "Long Term Effects of Divorce and Remarriage on the Adjustment of Children", *Journal of the American Academy of Child Psychiatry*, 24, 518-30.

Hetherington, E., Stanley-Hagan, M., and Anderson, E., (1989), "Marital Transitions: A Child's Perspective", *American Psychologist*, 44, 303-312.

Holman, R., (1980), "Exclusive and Inclusive Concepts of Fostering", in Triseliotis, J., *New Developments in Foster Care and Adoption*, London: Routledge and Kegan Paul.

Houghton Report, (1972), *Report of the Departmental Committee on the Adoption of Children*, London: HMSO, Cmnd. 5107.

Howe, D., Sawbridge, P., and Hinings, D., (1992), *Half a Million Women: Mothers Who Lose Their Children by Adoption*, London: Penguin.

Howell, D., and Ryburn, M., (1987), "New Zealand: New Ways to Choose Adopters", *Adoption and Fostering*, 11:4, 38-40.

Iwanek, M., (1987), "A Study of Open Adoption", 14 Emerson Street, Petone, Wellington, New Zealand: Unpublished.

Kadushin A, *Child Welfare Services*, 3rd ed , Toronto: MacMillan, 1980.

Kelly, G., and McCaulay, C., (1994), In preparation.

Kirk, D., (1964), *Shared Fate: A Theory of Adoption and Mental Health*, New York: Free Press.

Kirk, D., (1981), *Adoptive Kinship; A Modern Institution in Need of Reform,* Toronto: Butterworths.

Kirk, D., and McDaniel, S., (1984), "Adoption Policy in Great Britain and North America", *Journal of Social Policy*, 13 1, 75-84.

Kraft, A., Palombo, J., Woods, P., Mitchell, D., and Schmidt, A., (1985), "Some Theoretical Considerations on Confidential Adoptions, Part I, The Birth Mother", *Child and Adolescent Social Work*, 2 113-22.

Kraft, A., Palombo, J., Mitchell, D., Woods, P., and Tucker, N., (1985), "Some Theoretical Considerations on Confidential Adoptions, Part II, The Adoptive Parent", *Child and Adolescent Social Work*, 2 113-22.

Kraft, A., Palombo, J., Mitchell, D., Woods, P., Schmidt, A., and Tucker, N., (1985), "Some Theoretical Considerations on Confidential Adoptions, Part III, The Adopted Child", *Child and Adolescent Social Work*, 2 139-153.

Kraft, A., Palombo, J., Mitchell, D,.., Woods, P,.., Schmidt, A., and Tucker, N., "Some Theoretical Considerations on Confidential Adoptions, Part IV, Counter Transference", *Child and Adolescent Social Work,* 4, 1986, 3-14.

Kraft, A., Palombo, J., Mitchell, D., Dean, C., Meyers, S and Schmidt, A., "The Psychological Dimensions of Infertility", *American Journal of Orthopsychiatry*, 50, 618-628.

Lahti, J., (1982), "A Follow-up Study of Foster Children in Permanent Placements", *Social Service Review*, 56, 556-571, Chicago: University of Chicago.

Leeding, A., (1977), "Access to Birth Records", *Adoption and Fostering,* 89:3, 19-25.

Lifton, B., (1979), *Lost and Found: The Adoption Experience*, New York: Dial Press.

Lund, M., (1984), "Research on Divorce and Children", *Family Law*, 14, 198-201.

Maddox, B., (1980), *Step-Parenting*, London: Allen and Unwin.

McRoy, R., (1991), "American Experience and Research on Openness", *Adoption and Fostering*, 15:4, 99-110.

McRoy, R., Grotevant, H., and White, K., (1988), *Openness in Adoption: New Practices, New Issues*, New York: Praeger.

McWhinnie, A., (1967), *Adopted Children: How They Grow Up*, London: Routledge and Kegan Paul.

Meezan, W., and Shireman, J., (1982), "Foster Parent Adoption: A Literature Review", *Child Welfare*, 61, 525-535.

Menning, B., (1977), *Infertility: A Guide for the Childless Couple*, Englewood Cliff NJ: Prentice-Hall

Millham S., Bullock R., Hosie K., and Little M., *Lost in Care: the Problems of Maintaining Links Between Children in Care and their Families*, Aldershot: Gower 1986.

Mullender, A., (1991), "The Spread of Openness in New Zealand", in Mullender, A., [ed.], *Open Adoption: The Philosophy and the Practice*, London: BAAF.

Mullender, A., [ed.], (1991), *Open Adoption: The Philosophy and the Practice*, London: BAAF.

Raynor, L., (1980), *The Adopted Child Comes of Age*, London: George Allen and Unwin.

Rockel, J., and Ryburn, M., *Adoption Today: Change and Choice in New Zealand,* Auckland: Heinemann/Reed.

Rompf, E., (1993), "Open Adoption: What Does the "Average Person" Think?", Child Welfare, 72, 219-230.

Ross, H., and Milgram, J., (1982), "Important Variables in Adult Sibling Relationships: A Qualitative Study", in Lamb, M., and Sutton-Smith, B., [eds.], *Sibling Relationships: Their Nature and Significance Across the Lifespan*, Hillsdale NJ: Lawrence Erlbaum.

Ryburn, M., (1994, in preparation), "Adoptive Parents and Contested Adoption", in Ryburn, M., [ed.], *Contested Adoption Proceedings*, Aldershot: Gower/Arena.

Sachdev, P., (1991), "The Triangle of Fears: Fallacies and Facts", in Hibbs E., [ed], *Adoption: International Perspectives,* Madison CT: International Universities Press.

Sachdev, P., (1984), *Adoption: Current Issues and Trends*, Toronto: Butterworths.

Schaffer, H., (1990), *Making Decisions About Children: Psychological Questions and Answers*, Oxford; Basil Blackwell.

Schaffer, H., and Emerson, P., (1964), "Patterns of Response to Physical Contact in Early Human Development", *Journal of Child Psychiatry and Psychology*, 5, 1-13.

Shapiro, C., (1982), "The Impact of Infertility on the Marital Relationship", *Social Casework*, 63, 387-393.

Shawyer, J., (1979), *Death by Adoption*, Auckland: Cicada Press.

Short Report, (1984), *Second Report From the House of Commons Social Services Committee, "Children in Care",* London: HMSO.

Sorosky, A., Barran, A., and Pannor, R., (1975), "Identity Conflicts in Adoptees", *American Journal of Orthopsychiatry*, 45, 18-27.

Sorosky, A., and Pannor, R., (1978), *The Adoption Triangle*, New York: Doubleday/Anchor.

Stevenson, P., (1991), "A Model of Self Assessment for Prospective Adopters", *Adoption and Fostering*, 15:3, 20-27.

Thoburn, J., (1988), *Child Placement: Principles and Practice*, Wildwood House: London.

Thoburn, J., Murdoch, A., and O'Brien A., (1986), *Permanence in Child Care*, Oxford: Basil Blackwell, 1986.

Thoburn, J., (1989), *Success and Failure in Permanent Placement*, Avebury: Gower.

Thoburn, J, (1993), Personal communication, 21 October.

Tomlin Report, (1925), *First Report of the Child Adoption Committee*, London: British Parliamentary Papers, Cmnd., 2401.

Triseliotis, J., (1973), *In Search of Origins*, London: Routledge and Kegan Paul.

Valentine, D., [ed.], *Infertility and Adoption: A Guide for Social Work Practice*, New York: Harworth Press, 1990.

van Keppel, M., (1992), "Birth Parents and Negotiated Agreements", *Adoption and Fostering*, 15:4, 81-90.

Vernon, J., and Fruin, D., (1986), *In Care: A Study of Social Work Decision-Making*, London: National Children's Bureau.

Wallertstein, J., and Kelly, J., (1980), *Surviving the Break Up*, New York: Grant MacIntyre.

Wallerstein, J., and Blakeslee, S., (1989), *Second Chances,* London: Corgi 1989.

Wallerstein, J., Corbin, S., and Lewis, J., (1988), "Children of Divorce: A 10-Year Study", in Hetherington, E., and Arasteh, J., [eds.], *Impact of Divorce, Single Parenting, and Stepparenting on Children,* Hillsdale NJ: Erlbaum.

Watson, K., (1988), "The Case for Open Adoption", *Public Welfare,* 47, 24-28.

Wedge, P., and Mantle, G., (1991), *Sibling Groups in Social Work,* Aldershot: Gower, 1991.

Winkler, R., and van Keppel, M., (1984), *Relinquishing Mothers in Adoption: Their Long-Term Adjustment,* Melbourne: Institute of Family Studies, Monograph No., 3.

Introduction to part II
Howe, D., Sawbridge, P., and Hinings, D., (1992), *Half a Million Women: Mothers Who Lose Their Children by Adoption*, London: Penguin.

Rockel, J., and Ryburn, M., *Adoption Today: Change and Choice in New Zealand,* Auckland: Heinemann/Reed.

Chapter five: Lorette
Bouchier, P., Lambert, L., and Triseliotis, J., (1991), *Parting With a Child For Adoption: The Mother's Perspective,* London: BAAF.

Brinich, P., (1990), "Adoption, Ambivalence and Mourning", *Adoption and Fostering,* 14:1, 6-20.

Brodzinsky, D., Schechter, D., Braff, A., and Singer, L., (1984a), "Psychological and Academic Adjustment in Adopted Children", *Journal of Consulting and Clinical Psychology,* 52:4, 582-90.

Brodzinsky, D., Singer, L., and Braff, A., (1984b), "Children's Understanding of Adoption", *Child Development,* 55, 869-878.

Brodzinsky, D., Schechter, M., and Henig, R., (1992), *Being Adopted: The Lifelong Search for Self,* New York: Doubleday.

Cain, P., (1992), "Objectivity and Assessment", *Adoption and Fostering*, 16:2, 40-41.

Corcoran, A., (1991), "Opening of Adoption Records in New Zealand", in Hibbs, E., [ed.], *Adoption: International Perspectives*, Madison CT: International Universities Press.

Dominick, C., (1988), *Early Contact in Adoption: Contact Between Birth Mothers and Adoptive Parents at the Time of and After Adoption*, Research Series No 10, Wellington: Department of Social Welfare.

Field, J., (1991), "Views of New Zealand Birth Mothers on Search and Reunion", in Mullender, A., [ed.], *Open Adoption: The Philosophy and the Practice*, London: BAAF.

Fratter, J., Rowe, J., Sapsford, D., and Thoburn, J., (1991), *Permanent Family Placement: A Decade of Experience*, London: BAAF.

Griffith, K 91991), "Access to Records: The Results of the Changes in New Zealand Law", in Mullender, A., *Open Adoption: The Policy and the Practice*, London: BAAF.

Halsey, A., (1993), "Changes in the Family", *Children and Society*, 7:2, 125-136.

Henderson, M., (1990), "Shadow of Fear over Adoption", *The Guardian*, 12th September.

Howe, D., Sawbridge, P., and Hinings, D., (1992), *Half a Million Women: Mothers Who Lose Their Children by Adoption*, London: Penguin.

Howell, D., and Ryburn, M., (1987), "New Zealand: New Ways to Choose Adopters", *Adoption and Fostering*, 11:4, 38-40.

Jennings, N., (1992), "Adoption: Whose Needs Come First?", London: BBC II, *Open Space*, 1st June.

Kety, S., (1973), "Problems in Biological Research in Psychiatry", in Mendels, J., [ed.], *Biological Psychiatry*, London: Wiley.

Parkes C, *Bereavement: Studies of Grief in Adult Life*, Harmondsworth: Penguin, 1972.

Rockel, J., and Ryburn, M., *Adoption Today: Change and Choice in New Zealand*, Auckland: Heinemann/Reed.

Ryburn M, [ed.], (1994), in preparation, *Contested Adoption Proceedings*, Aldershot: Gower/Arena.

Ryburn M, (1991), "The Myth of Assessment", *Adoption and Fostering*, 15:1, 20-27.

Ryburn, M., (1992b), "The Myth of Assessment Revisited", *Adoption and Fostering*, 16:3, 3.

Sawbridge, P., (1990), "Post Adoption Services", Paper to BAAF Conference, *Adoption in the '90s*, Bristol, 2nd March.,

Short Report, (1984), *Second Report From the House of Commons Social Services Committee, 'Children in Care'*, London: HMSO.

Steinhauer, P., (1991), *The Least Detrimental Alternative: A Systematic Guide to Case Planning and Decision Making for Children in Care*, Toronto: University of Toronto Press.

Stevenson, P., (1991), "A Model of Self Assessment for Prospective Adopters", *Adoption and Fostering*, 15:3, 20-27.

White, R., (1991), "Adoption in a Framework of Child Welfare Legislation", in Hibbs, E., [ed.], *Adoption: International Perspectives*, Madison CT: International Universities Press.

Winkler, R., and van Keppel, M., (1984), *Relinquishing Mothers in Adoption: Their Long-Term Adjustment*, Melbourne: Institute of Family Studies, Monograph, No 3.

Chapter six: Joanne, Chris

Bateson, G., (1980), *Mind and Nature: A Necessary Unity,* New York: Bantam Books.

Bertocci, D., Schechter, M., (1991), "Adopted Adults' Perception of Their Need to Search: Implications for Clinical Practice", Smith Studies in Social Work, 61, 2, 179-196.

Bohman, M., (1978), "Some Genetic Aspects of Alcoholism and Criminality", *Archives of General Psychiatry*, 35, 269-276.

Cadoret, J., and Gath, A., (1978), "Inheritance of Alcoholism in Adoptees", *British Journal of Psychiatry*, 132, 252-258.

Etter, J., (1993), "Levels of Cooperation and Satisfaction in 56 Open Adoptions", *Child Welfare*, 72, 257-267.

Goodwin, D., Schulsinger, E., Moller, N., Hermansen, L., Winour, C., and Guze, S., (1974), "Drinking Problems in Adopted and Non Adopted Sons of Alcoholics", *Archives of General Psychiatry* , 31, 164-171.

Griffith, K., (1991), "Access to Records: The Results of the Changes in New Zealand Law", in Mullender, A., *Open Adoption: The Policy and the Practice*, London: BAAF.

Howe, D., Sawbridge, P., and Hinings, D., (1992), *Half a Million Women: Mothers Who Lose Their Children by Adoption*, London: Penguin.

Kirk, D., (1964), *Shared Fate: A Theory of Adoption and Mental Health*, New York: Free Press.

Kirk, D., (1981), *Adoptive Kinship; A Modern Institution in Need of Reform,* Toronto: Butterworths.

Rockel, J., and Ryburn, M., (1988), Adoption Today: Change and Choice in New Zealand, Auckland: Heinemann/Reed.

Ryburn, M., (1992a), "Advertising for Permanent Placements", *Adoption and Fostering,* 16:2, 8-15.

Ryburn, M, (1992b), "Contested Adoption Proceedings", *Adoption and Fostering,* 16:4, 28-38.

Ryburn, M., (1994, in preparation), "Birth Parents and Contested Adoption", in Ryburn, M., [ed.], *Contested Adoption Proceedings,* Aldershot: Gower/Arena.

Sachdev, P., (1991), "The Triangle of Fears: Fallacies and Facts", in Hibbs, E., [ed.], *Adoption: International Perspectives,* Maddison CT: International Universities Press.

Triseliotis, J., (1973), *In Search of Origins,* London: Routledge and Kegan Paul.

Chapter seven: Lois, Taff and Selina

Erikson, E., (1980), *Identity and the Life Cycle,* New York: Norton.

Fisher, M., Marsh, P., and Phillips, D., with Sainsbury, E., (1986), *In and Out of Care: the Experiences of Children, Parents and Social Workers,* London: Batsford/BAAF.

Ryburn, M., (1994, in preparation), "Birth Parents and Contested Adoption", in Ryburn, M., [ed.], *Contested Adoption Proceedings,* Aldershot: Gower/Arena.

Schaffer, H., (1990), *Making Decisions About Children: Psychological Questions and Answers,* Oxford: Basil Blackwell, 1990.

Vernon, J., and Fruin, D., (1986), *In Care: A Study of Social Work Decision-Making,* London: National Children's Bureau.

Chapter eight: Matthew and Annabel

Brodzinsky, D., Schechter, D., Braff, A., and Singer, L., (1984a), "Psychological and Academic Adjustment in Adopted Children", *Journal of Consulting and Clinical Psychology,* 52:4, 582-90.

Brodzinsky, D., Singer, L., and Braff, A., (1984b), "Children's Understanding of Adoption", *Child Development*, 55, 869-78.

Brodzinsky, D., Schechter, M., and Henig, R., (1992), *Being Adopted: The Lifelong Search for Self*, New York: Doubleday.

McMillan, R., and Hamilton, F., (1993), "Initiating Contact With Adoptive Families and Adopted People on Behalf of Birth Parents and Relatives", in *Adult Counselling and Adoption*, Burnell, A., Reich, D., and Sawbridge, P., [eds.], London: Post Adoption Centre/Barnardos.

Chapter nine: Lynne and Andrea

DoH, (1991), *Interdepartmental Review of Adoption Law, - The Nature and Effect of Adoption,* Paper 1, London: DOH.

Dominick, C., (1988), *Early Contact in Adoption: Contact Between Birth Mothers and Adoptive Parents at the Time of and After Adoption*, Research Series No 10, Wellington: Department of Social Welfare.

Etter, J., (1993), "Levels of Cooperation and Satisfaction in 56 Open Adoptions", *Child Welfare*, 72, 257-267.

Field, J., (1991), "Views of New Zealand Birth Mothers on Search and Reunion", in Mullender, A., [ed.], *Open Adoption: The Philosophy and the Practice*, London: BAAF.

Fisher, M., Marsh, P., Phillips, D., with Sainsbury, E., (1986), *In and Out of Care: The Experience of Children, Parents and Social Workers*, London: Batsford/BAAF.

Fox, N., (1977), "Attachment of Kibbutz Infants to Mothers and Metaplet", *Child Development,* 48, 1228-39.

Fratter, J., (1991), "Parties in the Triangle", *Adoption and Fostering*, 15:4, 91-98.

Fratter, J., (1989), *Family Placement and Access: Achieving Permanency for Children in Contact with Birth Parents,* Ilford: Barnardos.

Goldstein, J., Freud, A., and Solnit, A., (1973), *Beyond the Best Interests of the Child*, New York: Free Press.

Goldstein, J., Freud, A., and Solnit, A., (1979), *Before the Best Interests of the Child*, New York: Free Press.

Kirk, D., (1964), *Shared Fate: A Theory of Adoption and Mental Health*, New York: Free Press.

Kirk, D., (1981), *Adoptive Kinship; A Modern Institution in Need of Reform,* Toronto: Butterworths.

McRoy, R., (1991), "American Experience and Research on Openness", *Adoption and Fostering*, 15:4, 99-110.

Millham S., Bullock, R., Hosie, K., and Little, M., (1990), *Lost in Care: the Problems of Maintaining Links Between Children in Care and their Families*, Aldershot: Gower.

Millham, S., Bullock R., Hosie K., and Little M., *Access Disputes in Child-Care,* Aldershot: Gower, 1989.

Rowe, J., Cain, H., Hundleby, M., and Keane, A., (1984), *Long Term Foster Care,* London: Batsford/BAAF.

Rutter, M., (1980), *Maternal Deprivation Reassessed,* Harmondsworth: Penguin.

Schaffer, H., and Emerson, P., (1964), "Patterns of Response to Physical Contact in Early Human Development", *Journal of Child Psychiatry and Psychology*, 5, 1-13.

Trent, J., (1989), *Homeward Bound: The Rehabilitation of Children to Their Birth Parents*, Ilford: Barnardos.

Vernon, J., and Fruin, D., (1986), *In Care: A Study of Social Work Decision-Making*, London: National Children's Bureau.

Chapter ten: **Neil, Sarah, Robin, Charlotte, Maria, Marc, Gina**

Kirk, D., (1964), *Shared Fate: A Theory of Adoption and Mental Health*, New York: Free Press.

Kirk, D., (1981), *Adoptive Kinship; A Modern Institution in Need of Reform,* Toronto: Butterworths.

Rutter, M., (1980), *Maternal Deprivation Reassessed,* Harmondsworth: Penguin

Ryburn, M., (1991), "Openness and Adoptive Parents", in Mullender, A., [ed.], *Open Adoption: The Philosophy and the Practice*, London: BAAF.

Conclusion

Goffman, E., (1961), *Asylums: Essays in the Social Situation of Mental Patients and Other Inmates*, New York: Doubleday.

Kirk, D., (1964), *Shared Fate: A Theory of Adoption and Mental Health*, New York: Free Press.

Morgan, E., (1983), untitled poem in Johnston, P., [ed.], *Perspectives on a Grafted Tree*, Fort Wayne IN: Perspectives Press.

Triseliotis, J., (1973), *In Search of Origins*, London: Routledge and Kegan Paul.

Name index

Subject index